Intimate Partner Violence

Intimate Partner Violence

Reflections on Experience, Theory, and Policy

With an introduction by
SHARON BUTALA

Edited by
MARY RUCKLOS HAMPTON
and NIKKI GERRARD

✛ RESOLVE

Cormorant Books

ONTARIO ARTS COUNCIL
CONSEIL DES ARTS DE L'ONTARIO

The publisher gratefully acknowledges the support of the
Canada Council for the Arts and the Ontario Arts Council
for its publishing program. We acknowledge the financial support
of the Government of Canada through the Book Publishing
Industry Development Program (BPIDP) for our publishing activities.

Printed and bound in Canada

LIBRARY AND ARCHIVES CANADA CATALOGUING IN PUBLICATION

Intimate partner violence: reflections on experience, theory and
policy/edited by Mary Rucklos Hampton and Nikki Gerrard; with
an introduction by Sharon Butala.

Includes bibliographical references and index.

ISBN 1-896951-90-2

1. Family violence. I. Hampton, Mary Rucklos II. Gerrard, Nikki, 1947–

HV6626.I59 2006   362.82'92   C2005-904214-1

Cover design: Marijke Friesen
Cover image: Pillow Talk (wax on paper) © Teresa Posyniak
Text design: Tannice Goddard, Soul Oasis Networking
Printer: Canadian Printco Limited

CORMORANT BOOKS INC.
215 SPADINA AVENUE, STUDIO 230, TORONTO, ONTARIO, CANADA M5T 2C7
www.cormorantbooks.com

Contents

Her Husband Did That To Her

Sharon Butala

One afternoon a young mother, holding her new baby, and with her uncommunicative, slim young husband standing behind her, dropped in for a visit. I opened the door and exclaimed at once at her bruised cheek, cut lip, and faintly violet-coloured eye. *What happened to you?* I asked. She said that she had fallen downstairs. Ten years later, long after she and her family had moved across the country, one morning, some small item reminded me of her, and I remembered next, her bruised face. And suddenly, I realized what should have been obvious to me the long ago moment when I opened my door to her: *Her husband did that to her.* By that time, I could not remember her last name, nor had I any idea where she and her family had gone. Clearly, the opportunity for me to try to help, whether futile or not, was long past, and there was nothing now that I could do.

I will always wonder, had I recognized that bruising for what it was that very moment when I saw her face, could I have helped her then? And if I had tried, what would I have said to her? What might I have said to him? I did not know the answers to these questions, nor did I know why so young a man, a new husband, a new father, would assault the small young woman whom, only a year before, he had married. Was it because he was, as I've described him, uncommunicative? Unable to speak? And thus spoke in a way that could not be misunderstood? Or maybe he had been assaulted himself in his family home, or had grown used to seeing his father assault his mother, and accepted such violent behaviour as the norm. As for her, I could not imagine why she would accept being struck, and would even lie for him about it. As for the infant she held in her arms, how would that child be affected by seeing his mother struck by his father? Would his father soon extend his violent behaviour to him? Would the child himself eventually become an abuser? As a former teacher, I wondered too about how the fear and shame in which he was probably destined to live would affect his ability to learn in school, and to build a normal life for himself beyond it.

Then I thought about another woman I met when I lived in another province, and whose entire community knew that for years she was physically assaulted on a regular basis. It wasn't even a secret, and yet — although there may have been — I knew of no attempt to rescue her, or to stop the husband. I had heard people speak of the abused woman with contempt, because year after year she stayed, despite others telling her she should leave. And as for the three children in the home — the community did not hear that they too were handled violently by their father, but it seems unlikely that they were not.

I am hardly alone in such experiences with strangers or friends who have been assaulted by their husbands or boyfriends, and whose children are at risk, nor am I alone in the sense of helplessness to do anything to stop the abuse. The general public simply does not know what to do beyond calling the police, nor what to say to the woman who denies her abuse, or does not deny it, but insists on remaining in the family home despite it. Nor does the general public have any idea if, or how, abusers might be stopped and reclaimed for lives as decent citizens and worthy husbands and fathers.

That is why the research reported on in this volume is so desperately needed — so that these questions might be answered; so that the next step might be taken toward educating the public, the families of the abused, the well-meaning, but scolding or disgusted or angry friends as to an appropriate and helpful response. Beyond this, of course, the too-often tacit acceptance of family violence must be ended, so firmly, so finally, that even the most benighted individual abuser in this country can never again make excuses that anybody will listen to. Among these, police officers, judges and legislators should be the first.

RESOLVE is doing good work to this end, and this volume of reports is an excellent step toward educating all of us as to why this (to those of us never subjected to it) incomprehensible behaviour might occur, and what steps society might take to put an early end to it. Ending family violence is the huge job before us; our best hope resides in the efforts of these researchers and in agencies such as RESOLVE, which raises funds, identifies and supports such valuable work as is reported in this volume, and raises public awareness of the extent and degree of family violence and of its absolute unacceptability.

CHAPTER ONE

Introduction

Mary R. Hampton and Nikki Gerrard

The focus of this volume is adult women who experience Intimate Partner Violence (IPV). The term Intimate Partner Violence is meant to include all types of relationships; this gender-based phenomenon disproportionately affects women; all women are at risk and may experience abuse at any time in their lives (Mann, 2000; National Clearinghouse on Family Violence, 2004). Some chapters integrate theory and practice; others describe the experiences of the women who are victims of abuse and the anti-violence workers who advocate for them. At the time of writing these chapters, all the authors resided in the Canadian prairie provinces of Alberta, Manitoba, and Saskatchewan, but the chapters in this book will have relevance nationally and internationally for those with anti-violence agendas. The coherent theme that runs throughout all the chapters is the power of policy in the lives of our readers. The introductory chapter discusses the geographical context of the book; this is followed by a discussion about what policy is, the formation and application of policy, the impact of policy on victims of intimate partner abuse and anti-violence workers, and how good policies should be developed.

We believe this book will be of interest to women who have experienced intimate partner violence, service providers, academics, and policy-makers. This is the broad audience that RESOLVE (Research and

Education for Solutions to Violence and Abuse) addresses in its "slim volume" series. RESOLVE is a regional research network involving the three prairie provinces. All the projects supported by this network have in common the active participation of community- and university-based researchers and a commitment to produce results that are useful in policy and practice development as well as useful in academic settings (http://www.umanitoba.ca/resolve/). The network has expanded to include service providers, government policy-makers, and universities in the three provinces. This volume contains useful information for all these groups, keeping in mind RESOLVE's goal to influence policy and practice with an aim to eliminating violence in our society.

The Context: Canadian Prairies

The Canadian prairies are an important focus for research on intimate partner violence. National family violence trends reported by province reveal that Manitoba, Saskatchewan, and Alberta had the highest wife-homicide rates between 1976 and 1999 (Statistics Canada, 2001). Recent statistics released by the federal government suggest that rates of domestic violence in Canada overall are dropping slightly (Statistics Canada, 2004). This statistic does not reflect the situation of women on the prairies. Only Saskatchewan and Prince Edward Island reported increases in spousal-assault rates between 1993–1997. Admissions to shelters increased in Manitoba and Alberta, but decreased slightly in Saskatchewan. Saskatchewan and Manitoba had the largest increase in reports to police by female spousal violence victims in the period 1993–1999. This volume and previous volumes published in this series offer explanations and commentary on this trend (Ateah & Mirwaldt, 2004; Gorkoff & Runner, 2003; Hiebert-Murphy & Burnside, 2001; Proulx & Perrault, 2000; Tutty & Goard, 2002).

These rates of intimate partner violence on the prairies have implications for all our social systems, including the justice system and social services. For example, Saskatchewan and Alberta reported the greatest increase in use of social services by female spousal violence victims between 1993–1997 (Statistics Canada, 2001). There have been few detailed analyses of the structures of power and policy at the provincial level of

Canada, the level at which domestic violence policies are enacted (Wharf & McKenzie, 1998). The differential statistics cited above suggest a need to understand the unique impact of policy in each province.

Saskatchewan and Manitoba, particularly, comprise a large rural and farm population (Statistics Canada, 1996). The changing social, political, and economic factors that affect all aspects of rural life also influence the policies that support or hinder the efforts of anti-violence workers. Hornosty and Doherty (2002), and Robertson (1998) conclude that it is crucial to recognize the unique needs of women who reside in rural and farm communities and that a variety of social and cultural factors hinder abused women's access to services and resources, while economic conditions in rural areas limit options for women to become financially independent. Federal and provincial government plans for economic diversification, as well as for delivery of health care, education, justice, and other services, must be designed and evaluated with an eye to assessing their impact on abused rural and farm women.

What is Policy?

Every chapter refers to policies that affect women who are abused by intimate partners. "Policy" is one of those terms we assume we understand but in fact find hard to define. According to Wharf and McKenzie (1998), "social policy is synonymous with public policy and encompasses all of the actions of governments and their continuing but not always consistent attempts to regulate social and economic structures in a citizen's quality of life" (p. 9). Policy is intended to guide decisions when choice of direction is "clouded by conflicting values and where facts and information cannot be marshalled to establish clearly that one choice is superior to all others" (Wharf & McKenzie, 1998, p. 10). In other words, policies are principles developed at all levels (global, governmental, provincial, local, institutional) to guide our choice of action. Unfortunately, policies are more often influenced by economic matters than guided by the well-being of all citizens. Policies are also influenced by individual and collective ideologies and beliefs. Ursel (1992) documents the history of the transition from familial to social patriarchy and the ways that state intervention (policy) has been used to harm as well as help women's causes. We suggest that policy is power and that those in charge of making policy are not always those most affected by policy.

The Formation and Application of Policy

Women abused by intimate partners, and the anti-violence workers who fight for them, have little voice in policy direction. Coleman and Skogstad (1990) equate the women's movement with the poverty community in their level of power and influence: both are subjects of much public policy-discourse, but neither has had much impact on policy development. Wharf and McKenzie (1998) describe the disconnect between those who make policy and those who implement it: "In the social services, men have assumed most of the policy-making roles, and women have assumed most of the responsibility for implementation" (p. 21), even though these policies have disproportionately affected women. Wharf and McKenzie also found that policy directives from head office were seldom adequate responses to the needs of service users.

When the word "policy" is used, most of us imagine that the important policy decisions are made by governments and that we have little influence over these decisions. The literature is focused mostly on macro-level policies at the federal government level without providing insight into the policy-making processes relevant to the human services that could be transposed to provincial and non-governmental sectors. Wharf and McKenzie (1998) argue that attention to the principle of inclusiveness in Wharf and McKenzie's generating policy is the single most important reform needed in the human services. Policies that exclude the knowledge of those who receive services and those who implement services will be incomplete and inappropriate. Wharf and McKenzie's vision for inclusive policy development requires participation of a role-model/practitioner who exemplifies the respectful, consumer-centred professional.

The Impact of Policy on Victims of Violence and Anti-Violence Workers

Many of the authors in this book talk about the impact of policies (or lack thereof) on the victims of violence or anti-violence workers.

Experiences of Women

Leslie Tutty presents narratives from 41 Alberta women who have gone to emergency shelters or have been involved with the police. Her data debunk many myths about the phenomenon of intimate partner abuse, myths that can influence policy development. She focuses particularly on firearm utilization as an aspect of intimate partner abuse, bringing the private fear that many women live with into the public domain. Society must understand that intimate partner violence is not simply marital conflict taken to an extreme, but, rather, it is a profoundly different phenomenon. Sharing their experiences of abuse, her participants help us understand the complex and horrific nature of intimate partner violence. Tutty highlights the fact that policies must focus the responsibility for the abuse on the abusers, not on the women who were subjected to it.

According to Nayyar Javed, immigrant and refugee women need policies that have been based in part on awareness of these women's credentials and skills, so that if she is abused, a woman can find a way to support herself financially. The silencing of abused immigrant and refugee women is partly due to government policies that no longer provide support for building the capacity of these women's organizations, thus leaving them isolated.

Theories and Their Link to Intervention

Carmen Gill argues for the importance of understanding different theoretical perspectives because they provide the lenses through which different intervention strategies are viewed. Woman abuse is not gender-neutral and must be named and viewed as a problem of violence against women. Gender-neutral language has had a negative impact on policy implementation, from the perspective of women who experience intimate partner abuse. Gill offers a thorough review of dominant theories used to explain woman abuse, focusing specifically on Canadian literature. She critiques the micro/individual-level theories, suggesting they inadequately explain the phenomenon. Macro/societal-level explanations, on the other hand, bring this once "private" issue into the public and political arena. Feminist theory offers the most promising approach for framing intervention strategies because it is focused on women's experiences, includes critique of existing ideologies and institutional systems, and holds great potential for social change.

One Approach to Intervention

Karen Nielsen and Ann Marie Dewhurst have worked for many years both with men who abuse their intimate partners and with these partners. They have found that women who survive abuse have knowledge that can help women with safety planning; using this information, they have developed a model. The Harm Reduction and Abused Women's Safety Framework will be a helpful resource for service providers, policy-makers, and women who experience intimate partner abuse. Their chapter provides important insights on developing policies for intervening in appropriate ways at helpful times. The model includes information about the steps involved when women are attempting to make changes in their lives and about barriers likely to be encountered in the change process, and has suggestions for appropriate interventions at each stage of choice.

Aboriginal Women's Experience of Justice Policies

Jane Ursel describes interventions that may help Aboriginal women, who are more at risk of abuse than non-Aboriginal women. She writes, "The only way to reduce the over-representation of Aboriginal people is to respond to Aboriginal women's calls for help differently than non-Aboriginal women" (Ursel, this volume). Ursel advocates for consistent treatment by police in cases of intimate partner violence. She paints a picture of the way Aboriginal women experience violence and encounter the justice system after the violence has occurred, starting with policing through to the court system.

What Interventions Can Prevent Femicide

Deb Farden's list of policies, if put in place, would decrease or perhaps eliminate femicide. These policies, which include mandatory reporting of witnessed violence and enhanced communication links between agencies, are focused on a women-centred approach, promotion of advocacy for abused women and their children, education of men about their violence, the need to act on the fears of women, the imperative of investigating and taking seriously previous criminal charges, elimination of legal delays, and the need for parole boards to listen to anonymous requests to deny an abuser parole.

The Experience of Anti-Violence Workers

In Stephanie Martin's chapter, she highlights the need for workplace policies to assist anti-violence workers, who are susceptible to secondary traumatic stress. Awareness of how being exposed, day in and day out, to stories about violence can create extreme distress for these listeners needs to be coupled, Martin suggests, with policies that allow workers to take time off, get support, or reduce their workload for a period of time.

Anti-Violence Workers Critique Policies

According to participants in Mary Hampton's study, the two factors that are most important in supporting women leaving abusive relationships are: (1) legal support and (2) economic self-sufficiency (a finding similar to Gelles' 1976 conclusions). Hampton states that existing policies clearly undermine achievement of these two factors. The problem of intimate partner violence cuts across many systems; because of this, women who need help can fall through the cracks or find it impossible to negotiate the complexities of differing systems.

As you will read in the chapters in this book, violence against women is a result of the fundamental ideology of the patriarchal system we live in, so much an engrained part of the fabric of our society that it is invisible to policy-makers. However, as one participant in Hampton's interviews stated, "Violence against women is in epidemic proportions in our country." DeKeseredy and Ellis (1995) conclude that many of the policies that currently exist will not, in the long run, eliminate the deeper roots of intimate partner violence, which are grounded in structural economic inequalities and patriarchal ideologies.

Developing Good Policies About Intimate Partner Violence

Wharf and McKenzie (1998) advocate a participatory approach to policy-making that includes practitioners and service users. Many authors in this book note that neither people who work with abused women nor the victims themselves are ever consulted about the development of policies relating to violence. Front-line practitioners, working collaboratively with service users and policy-makers, could make important contributions to the policy-making process.

Policies about intimate partner violence need to be based partly on such contextual factors as geographical isolation and/or immigrant or refugee status. There are various areas in this work that need good policies: victims, anti-violence workers, shelters for abused women, and workplaces where anti-violence work is done. Those who develop policy should not be far removed from those who implement it.

We felt that by beginning with women's lived experience with violence, then exploring theoretical concepts, introducing a variety of interventions, learning about the impact of violence on anti-violence workers and the importance of participatory policy-making, we could provide a practical, insightful, and helpful resource to address and eradicate intimate partner violence.

CHAPTER TWO

There But for Fortune:
How Women Experience Abuse by Intimate Partners

Leslie M. Tutty

Society has been slow to acknowledge the serious nature of woman abuse, despite the advocacy of representatives from women's shelters and the research from the past 30 years that has documented the dynamics of intimate partner violence. Canadian national studies such as the 1999 General Social Survey included important questions not only about the extent to which individuals reported being injured and abused by partners but also the effects on them of injury and fear for their lives (Tutty & Goard, 2002).

It is important to bear witness to this abuse in order to raise awareness of the hidden and serious nature of the violence and its impact on women, children and families. It can be difficult for the general public to understand that abuse is not simply marital conflict taken to an extreme; it is profoundly different. Resolving marital disputes effectively is part of the process of living successfully with intimate partners. Abuse, on the other hand, is intentionally harmful, is targeted at one's partner's vulnerabilities, is ongoing, and is often not related to marital issues at all. The violence is significantly out of proportion to any precipitating incident.

What do we know of the experiences of women who have survived abusive relationships? What evidence is there that woman abuse warrants the network of shelters across Canada and the attentions of numerous legal, social services and counselling organizations? What do women who have not been abused have in common with women who have endured what to most of us seems unendurable?

In this chapter I present narratives from 41 Alberta women who had either sought refuge in emergency shelters or were involved with the police because their partners had assaulted them or threatened their lives with firearms (Tutty, 1999a). The women describe their relationships, at what point they became aware they were being abused, and how they resisted and tried to understand the abuse. They recount the impact on themselves and their children and the traumatic nature of the abuse they experienced. Only a few of the women could have predicted that they would be abused, suggesting our commonalities rather than our differences.

Myths about Women Abused by Intimate Partners

While the research on intimate partner violence and its effects on women is vast, we have created new myths that categorize these women as victims, as somehow uniquely different from ourselves. The early research on intimate partner violence largely focused on the women's characteristics that might answer the question, "why do they stay in abusive relationships?" This not-so-subtle portrayal of abused women as masochistic has seemingly been dismissed and characterized as blaming the victim (for further critical discussion on women and masochism, see Caplan, 1985). However, the issue of why women stay with abusive partners remains a question for the general public and even for professionals who deal with such assaults. I recently heard a lawyer asking a woman in court why she didn't leave her partner. His tone and manner implied the abuse was her fault, almost a direct quote from the writings of the 1980s. The idea that there is something implicitly wrong with women who do not leave assaultive partners has not vanished.

Many women are committed to abusive partners and do not leave after being abused once or even over a considerable time: breaking away from any intimate relationship is always complicated and normally requires time (Rothery, Tutty & Weaver, 1999). However, the most commonly cited statistics, about the number of times women return to abusive partners after shelter stays, are dated: women average four or five attempts to leave partners before a permanent separation (Giles-Sims, 1983; Okun, 1988). A more recent study with 64 Alberta shelter residents found that 90 percent were living independently after six months to a year after their shelter stay (Tutty & Rothery, 2002).

Other researchers studied whether having witnessed one's father abusing one's mother is correlated with women being victimized by their partners. Research on the "intergenerational transmission of abuse" has been relatively common, and looks at the extent to which both men and women might be living out patterns modeled by their parents. In 1990, Hotaling and Sugarman summarized a substantial body of research on battered women, stating that not one characteristic of the women explained either why they became involved with assaultive men or stayed in abusive marriages. An updated review of similar studies (Tutty, 1999b) supports the conclusion that, while a large proportion of abusive men, as children, often observed their fathers abusing their mothers, the same is not true for women. Interestingly, though, the intergenerational transmission of abuse is still commonly applied to women as to men.

The women are often portrayed as moving from abusive partner to abusive partner, implying that not only have they had abusive liaisons in the past, but also that after leaving a currently assaultive partner, they are seen as vulnerable to forming new relationships with men who will subsequently abuse them. Furthermore, partner abuse is often believed to be a phenomenon typical to people from the lower class, with little education and few job skills. Current research documents that women from all socio-economic classes are abused (Roberts, 2002).

Researchers have also focused on the impact on women of intimate partner abuse, looking at the symptoms that they commonly report as problematic. Coping with an abusive relationship creates considerable anxiety, especially if the threats and physical abuse continue over time (Tutty & Goard, 2002). Abused women often experience low self-esteem, anxiety, depression, suicidal ideation and substance abuse (Tutty, 1998). However, these are best seen as the result of living in an assaultive relationship, rather than as predisposing factors to entering into such partnerships; nor should they commonly be interpreted as the woman having a mental health disorder herself (Gondolf, 1998).

Since considerable research has documented the traumas and negative consequences for women who live with abusive partners, we are at risk of perceiving these women as victims, not seeing their strengths and coping abilities to both endure abuse and, ultimately, decide to leave. What do we know of the lives of these women beyond their victimization? How did they become involved with men who ultimately assaulted and denigrated them so severely? How did they cope and what are the strengths that allowed them to survive such abuse? What can we learn from them that we can apply to our own intimate relationships? This chapter focuses on these questions.

Introducing the Research and the Women Respondents

The purpose of the research was to explore ways in which firearms are used by abusive partners, since the risk of homicide is much greater when such weapons are involved (Campbell, Sharps & Glass, 2000). The following narratives are from a study conducted in Alberta with forty-one women, whose partners had either threatened them or had assaulted them with firearms, as one aspect of the relationship violence (Tutty, 1999a). I contacted the women through shelters in which they had stayed or through the specialized police teams which had assisted them. Virtually no literature has focused on firearm utilization as a component of intimate partner abuse.

The women were an average age of 37 years (range of 19 to 53) when we interviewed them. Most were Caucasian (33 or 81 percent), seven (16 percent) were Aboriginal or Métis, and one was Middle Eastern. Two of the women had immigrated to Canada within the past decade (one from the Middle East and one from the Ukraine); the rest were Canadian-born.

The women were primarily married to (66 percent) or lived common-law with (30 percent) the partner that abused them. Only two women (5 percent) were dating the men who had assaulted them; in both cases these were relatively short relationships, after the women had been married previously. In one unique circumstance, a woman was abused by an acquaintance of her husband from her country of origin, who, as is the practice in her culture, was essentially treated as a member of the family. He sexually assaulted her and then threatened her life and the lives of her children if she told anyone.

Except for the women who were dating, the relationships averaged 10 years, with a range of 8 months to 33 years. At the time that we interviewed the women, only two were still living with the partner who had threatened/used firearms against them. In one case, the incident had occurred a number of years previously and his abusive behaviour had decreased substantially. Another woman returned to care for her ex-husband when he became very ill. Three women had only recently left their partners to seek safety in an emergency shelter. Whether they would return to the relationships was not yet entirely clear, although when interviewed none intended to go back.

That most of the respondents had left their assaultive partners is typical of many studies with abused women. Note, however, that their narratives may not represent the experiences of women who continue to reside with abusive intimate partnerships.

This was the first marital or common-law relationship for 24 women (64 percent). The other 14 had previously been in long-term relationships (13 married and one common-law). Of these previous liaisons, most (11 or 79 percent) had not been abusive; only 3 women had been abused by previous partners — contrary to the myth that abused women go from one abusive relationship to another.

The majority of the women (37 of 41, or 90 percent) had children, whose ages ranged from 3 to 33 years of age. Four women (10 percent) had no children; 6 (15 percent) had 1 child; 22 (54 percent) had 2 or 3; and 9 women (22 percent) had 4 to 7 children.

In terms of education, 9 women (22 percent) had not completed high school; 3 women (7 percent) had completed up to Grade 8; 6 (15 percent) had some high school. Of the remainder, about a third were high school graduates (32 percent); a quarter had some university or college courses (24 percent); and another quarter had college or university degrees (22 percent). In summary, 32 women (78 percent) were high school graduates or above, a highly educated group. Two-thirds of the women were working when interviewed (27 or 66 percent). Of these, 8 (20 percent) were employed in clerical or retail jobs, and 9 (22 percent) worked in technical areas as chemical or engineering technicians or teaching assistants. Ten of the women (24 percent) were professionals, including 4 nurses, a chemist and an engineer.

With respect to their sources of income, 18 women (44 percent) had full-time jobs and another 2 worked part-time. Seventeen were residing in either emergency or second-stage shelters when interviewed, so were more likely to be living on social assistance, as they were in transition from abusive relationships. Nevertheless, two residents maintained their jobs during their shelter stay and two were students. Six non-shelter residents were also receiving social assistance: two were starting job-training in the near future and one was caring for a special-needs child. One woman received disability support for a medical condition.

There was a mix of women who resided in rural, compared to urban, centres when they were involved with abusive partners. Twenty-one women (51 percent) lived exclusively in rural centres, 17 (42 percent) lived exclusively in urban areas and 3 (7 percent) lived in a mix of locations with more time spent in rural communities.

The Abusive Partners

The background information on the male partners was gathered from the women. Some was incomplete or possibly inaccurate, since the women are not always given details about the partner's past or current activities, nor were they necessarily told the truth.

The majority of the men (thirty-one) were Caucasian (76 percent), nine were Aboriginal (22 percent) and one (2 percent) was non-white from a Middle-Eastern country. The men averaged 42 years of age (ranging from 25 to 65). They were, on average, statistically significantly older than their partners ($t = 6.03$; $p = 0.00$). In terms of education, 20 percent of the men had completed below or up to Grade 8; about one-quarter (27 percent) had some high school; 15 percent were high school graduates; 12 percent had some college/university courses or were graduates. In comparison with the women, the men had less formal education, although not to a statistically significant degree.

The men were employed in a range of jobs. One-third (38 percent, or 14 men) worked as labourer/construction workers; one-quarter (24 percent or nine men) owned their own business or were consultants; five (14 percent) were technicians or semi-skilled workers; five (14 percent) were farmers; two (5 percent) were professionals; and two were solely involved in criminal activities such as drug dealing. Work information was missing on four men. Two partners were police officers and two were veterans of the

Vietnam War with special assault weapons training.

Of the 36 men for whom the women had information on work status, most worked full-time (59 percent or 23 men); five (13 percent) were unemployed and looking for work; five (13 percent) worked part-time. Five (13 percent) were on disability for health problems such as post-traumatic stress syndrome or heart conditions, and one (3 percent) was on social assistance.

In looking at previous relationships, the women reported that eighteen (56 percent) of the men had not been in long-term live-in partnerships before. Of the rest, 13 men (40 percent) were known to have been abusive to a previous partner; 1 was known not to have been abusive. Information about previous partners was not available from nine women.

Meeting the Abusive Partner

With several exceptions, detailed later, the women met their partners in the same way as do most of us: at school, work or in pubs or bars. Many were introduced by family or friends. The majority met their partners when in their 20's. The following are quotes from women whose intimate partners were their first serious relationships:

> I met him through a friend. I had a fairly dysfunctional childhood, so didn't know what I should expect in a relationship. I met him in 1986. I was 25. He's four years older. He's a civil engineer, so [we're] both post-secondary people. We did really well. We had our own home; what we needed we went and got.

> We met at a local bar. My mom was with me. She was the one who gave him the phone number. I told her that I wasn't interested. I never wanted anyone that drank. He called me up a week after. Me and my mom and my brothers were getting ready to go on a picnic, and she invited him. It happened from that picnic. He was a good supporter at first, real supportive towards me and my family.

> In a country bar. We started talking right away and told each other our life story. He had this beautiful picture of the farm and how wonderful it was, six children. I thought that was quite nice

> because I'm from a big family and we're close. He was the man of
> my dreams.
>
> I went out with a really good friend ... I was working through the
> day and evenings, waitressing and going to school, so it was hard
> to get together with friends. She begged me to go out on a Sunday
> night, which I never do, so I went out with her. There was this
> really nice-dressed guy, dark hair, brown eyes, and when he started
> walking towards us, I thought he was going to ask her to dance,
> and he asked me. It started from there.

Each of the five women whose relationships started when they were in their
early teens but which lasted over ten years, had distinctive stories about
meeting their partners:

> I walked into a store and he was the manager, very outgoing. It was
> the trendiest store in town and they always had tickets to every-
> thing and we always went everywhere. I started going out with him
> when I was 14. [What was in it for him?] The sex, obviously, which
> is probably all he was interested in. I had a different background
> than he did, I always dressed nicely and he could see that. It's not
> hard to figure out what he saw in a 14-year-old.
>
> He was from the same town, a very small town, about 1,500 people.
> He's a lot older than me. I knew him from when I was really young,
> but we started dating when I was about 16. We were legally mar-
> ried when I was 24. [According to a referral source, her partner was
> originally her mother's live-in partner, who then began sexually
> abusing her.]

Another 12 women had previously been married or lived in long-term
common-law relationships. Most had children from their first marriages
although not all of the children currently lived with them. The women
provided the following descriptions of meeting their new partners who
ultimately became abusive:

He was a finishing carpenter and I met him through my friend. She thought that I should be with somebody. She phoned and said that I should come to the lake. He looked like my brother and that's why she liked him ... she liked my brother.

I met a Canadian man in the Ukraine. He said he had his own business for 30 years in Canada. He was 16 years older, a friend of my mother and father. It was a friendly meeting with my sister and the Canadian man who introduced us and a few other people. He asked if I would show him the city the next time he was there, the historical places. He was a Ukrainian-Canadian; he had the same blood as I. I agreed ... there was nothing wrong. He looked very polite.

We met through the Internet. It's interesting when you look back if you've learned about abusive relationships. He was very charming. When we met, I didn't have any children living with me and I was working. I had a good job; I was just lonely and wanted to meet somebody. He appeared very stable because he's worked at the same place for 25 years, a shift coordinator at a warehouse, so he appeared very stable, and I was looking for a relationship.

While most of the narratives of meeting partners were banal and non-descript, several women met men who sounded potentially dangerous from the beginning:

He sort of latched onto me when I was 15 and I couldn't shake him. When I was in high school, I continued to date other people hoping he'd get the picture, but he didn't get it, He's the same age as me. He decided that I was his and that was it. It wasn't really a relationship, I was walking home from a school dance and he came up with a van, his dad's van. I didn't get a chance to get away from him. He took me to a gravel pit and raped me at gun point.

I had an accident and ended up with a broken neck; I was overseas. He looked after me; he was very kind. He'd been bad to other people, but I never thought he'd be bad to me. I knew he was a pretty bad boy, but I didn't want to know. The less you know, the less you can get hurt, right? My friends just loved him; they thought he was wonderful. He was Mr. Charming. A couple of days later, he said, "Let's get married." I thought, maybe he wants to start afresh.

I went there to score [drugs]. He said, "OK, you can come back any time" ... it was like a joke. We all started laughing. A week later, I got a phone call and he said, "I really want to get to know you better." I said, "Do you want to come out here?" I was thinking next week and he said, "I can be there in an hour." It happened that fast, boom! I can say in hindsight that I just gave him permission to take control. Right from that day, he took control. I would do exactly what he said. I should quit nursing my baby. She was old enough to be on the bottle or on the cup. She was four or five months old.

The Genesis of the Abuse

On meeting their partners, most of the women in the study had no, if any, indicators that the men would become abusive. This section documents the points at which the women, sometimes in retrospect, recognized the serious nature of some of their partners' behaviour. In a number of instances, the abusive behaviour began shortly after the relationship started:

If I looked back now, it would be all the typical stuff; his very dysfunctional background, his control of the money. He wanted to buy a horse and gave me $50 for a month's groceries. Do it my way or else there's a big fight.

He became abusive shortly after they became a couple. He was possessive, jealous, called her names, put her down. He was physically abusive as well, pushing her down, grabbing and being rough with her. She had no serious injuries from the physical abuse. [Interview notes]

Right away. It was more emotional and verbal abuse at the beginning, more controlling behaviour. I wasn't allowed to have friends, wasn't allowed to have anything to do with my family.

For other women the change was gradual:

Within the first year, the disagreements became physical and sometimes he seemed angry about things that weren't that significant or were personal choices. [Was he hitting or pushing you?] Yes. [Did it become worse?] Over the course of the nine years, yes; but not rapidly or necessarily consistently.

My ex-husband was really good for the first four or five years. Couldn't have asked for a nicer guy; [he'd] do anything for you. Then all of a sudden, he left for work one day, and I don't know who came back in, but it was somebody else and that person never left again. [What do you think happened?] I haven't got a clue. I have tried to figure that out for years! He wasn't a boozer; he wasn't a druggie. I don't know what changed. I think it was I was getting more independent. He couldn't control me. I've always been the type that's been very hard to control. I like a relationship 50-50; I don't want it all one-sided. I want to be able to use my brain too. And I think he wanted to start controlling. He was trying to do it bit by bit and I was fighting him along the way, not letting him control the situation.

My husband and I were married for four years. The incidents of verbal and physical abuse gradually increased to a fairly significant proportion. I worked and was dealing with the public, but had somehow managed to hide this from everyone. Nobody really knew the truth. My [partner], as well, was a professional. During the relationship when incidents occurred, I loved him and he knew exactly how to push my buttons as far as turning on the charm. After he'd done it, he'd bring me flowers and treat me like a queen. I'd fall for it every time. I don't think that I'm stupid; it's got nothing to do with intelligence. It's got to do with lack of self-esteem. You think

> that you can't live without them. The guy told you that you're ugly and fat ... who'd want you anyways?

Several women had lived common-law with their partners for substantial periods. They identified the abuse as beginning immediately after they became legally married. Such a shift suggests that after marriage the men perceived their wives differently, more as possessions, supporting a feminist view of abuse as reflecting patriarchal attitudes towards women.

> I've been with this guy for two years. Well, actually six years. I've been married to him for two. I'd never seen that side of him until the ring was on my finger. Then it was a whole different story. He shook the baby. He picked him up and shook him because he couldn't handle his crying because he was fussing.

> It was like he removed his mask after our marriage ... after the kindness, the beautiful promises. "I'll make you the happiest woman in the world; show you the whole world." He said to my mother, my son, "Don't worry. She will be safe with me. She will be happy." After our marriage, he started to torment me, abuse me.

> I thought it would be better after we got married because he was so insecure because he was older than me; he was quite overweight, and always so scared I would find somebody younger. I thought if we got married, it would make him more secure, but it didn't; it just made it worse; I don't know why.

As has been well-documented by a number of studies (Campbell, 1998), the abuse began for some women when they became pregnant:

> The controlling part started after I got pregnant with my first son. That's when it all started. He never wanted me to go anywhere or visit with anyone. He'd get really mad and start storming around the house. All of a sudden, he was drinking and that's when the abuse started.

After only two months, he pushed her down the stairs. She was pregnant and lost the baby. A month later she became pregnant again and they stayed together. She considered the emotional abuse worse than the physical. He called her "slut," "cunt," "whore" and constantly criticized her. He would grab her by the hair and throw her around. [Interviewer Notes]

> It could be because I got pregnant right away. He went progressively worse, but really fast. It started where he would punish himself by punching brick walls on the outside, or playing a game where he wouldn't come in. He'd stay on my porch all night. It'd be rainy and cold but he wouldn't come in. And it didn't take long until it got worse. He didn't like my friends and that got uncomfortable. All of a sudden I was alone. Then he started yelling and throwing things.
>
> He raped me once before I got pregnant with my oldest daughter. All through the pregnancy he abused me and six months into it [it was] stillborn. I blamed myself.
>
> Things started feeling not right as soon as I got pregnant. For one thing, when I did tell him I was pregnant, he accused me of purposely getting pregnant. When I think back now, there were signs. I didn't know it was going to turn into all this.

Several respondents noted that the first serious abuse was directed to their children:

> The first rage was when my child was one and a half years. That was the first rage and it was directed toward the child ... no physical contact, but the actual rage was directed at the child. He's what I call a random rager. He could rage two to three times a year or two to three times a month. There's no provocation, no pattern. There's a way to lessen the rages I've only noticed over the last five years when the rages got worse: submitting to sex.

> I've seen him be violent with my son, twice. Gave him stitches, and
> rolled up the car window on his neck. It was one of those automat-
> ics. My son was sitting in the back seat, looked out the window. He
> [partner] was mad at us. My son couldn't breathe. So that never left
> me. I tried to smooth things over, but as the years went by, he [part-
> ner] started not wanting me to have anything to do with my kids.

Explaining their Partners' Abusive Behaviours

As the relationships proceeded, the women learned more of their partners'
characteristics and backgrounds that could explain the abuse. These explanations parallel what researchers have examined in attempting to understand
why men would behave violently to women partners. One possibility
is that the men are generally violent and have criminal backgrounds
(Kaufman-Kantor & Jasinski, 1998). Twenty-three men (56 percent) in the
current study had previously been charged with criminal offences, excluding
assaults against their partner. Nine spent time in jail for these non-spouse
assaults — the terms ranged from six months to ten years. Four men received
jail terms for robbery, three for assault (one against a police officer), one for
drinking and driving, and one for drug dealing. In four of these, the prison
sentence was completed a number of years ago:

> He started getting involved with some really unsavoury people
> years ago. [Criminal types?] Yeah. He said if I ever went to the
> police I would end up dead.

> He got a five year prison sentence and he only did five months. I
> knew prison wouldn't help. He [partner] was still making money.
> He was still dealing drugs when he came out. He had other people
> dealing drugs for him. He was still making money, even though he
> was in there [prison].

The women did not necessarily know about their partners' criminal histories: many of the charges were laid before the relationships began. Some
women learned of previous charges only after they had called the police or
left the relationship. One woman learned that her husband was wanted by

Interpol a year after he left her and Canada. She and another respondent also learned after separating that their husbands were still legally married to previous partners.

Although alcohol is involved in a substantial proportion of abuse incidents, it is not generally regarded as causing intimate partner violence (Roberts, 2002). However, over half the women in the current study (22 or 55 percent) considered their partners to have serious substance-abuse problems:

> He held a shotgun to my head when he was really drunk. I guess you only have to have that happen once in your lifetime to know what it feels like. I just kind of froze. If someone's sober and pulls a gun on you, that's scary enough, but what if he's stumbling ...

> He'd have his brothers over drinking. They'd start talking about hunting and he'd get his gun. He'd start pointing and waving it around. [What would he point it at?] Me. [He would point it at you in front of his brothers?!] Yes. He wouldn't let us [she and her four and six year old sons] go to sleep when he was drinking. He always insisted that we had to stay right there when he was drinking.

However, another 18 (45 percent) respondents did not consider that their partners abused substances. Several women commented that their partners were always completely sober when abusing them:

> He didn't have a drinking problem. For all exterior purposes, he's your upstanding citizen, middle-high income range, clean, well dressed, nice home.

Her partner dealt drugs in school. He had a small hydroponics operation in the house but he neither drank nor used substances. His abuse was done stone sober.

Other theorists have tried to link spousal violence to the men having mental health problems such as antisocial personality disorder (Dutton & Golant, 1995) or head traumas (Rosenbaum, Hoge, Adelman, Warnken

Fletcher & Kane, 1994). Almost one-third of the men (13 or 32 percent) in this study had been treated or received psychiatric attention. Six men were diagnosed as depressed, three were described as having an antisocial personality disorder, and two were diagnosed as having a bipolar disorder. One, a veteran of the Vietnam War, was receiving treatment for post-traumatic stress disorder and also displayed paranoid tendencies, and another had violent, paranoid thoughts after a serious head injury.

> [Partner] kept telling me that I should see a shrink because there was something wrong with my head. I made an appointment with this fellow I'd heard about through my friend. I talked to him for about 15 minutes and he said, "You're not nuts, but your husband is." He said he was a psychopath. A sociopath has no knowledge of what they're doing is wrong; a psychopath knows. He [partner] knew full well and enjoyed doing it. He was a psychopath.

> Very violent, very sick. That's why I just wanted to get out of there. He's a very sick person — I don't know if he's paranoid, psychotic, he thinks that there's other men coming into the house who I'm having affairs with.

The Nature of the Abuse Throughout the Relationship

It is difficult to portray the ongoing and all-encompassing nature of the abuse experienced by the women, especially when simply looking from one vignette to another. This section provides an overview of the overlap of kinds of abuse that the women disclosed.

The men emotionally abused all the women. Just over half the women (23 or 56 percent) noted that their partners were extremely jealous and imagined, almost always unjustifiably, that the women were having affairs. The most extreme example of this was a man who checked his wife's private parts when she came home, and insisted that she could only bathe with him, not alone. For almost one-third of the respondents (13 women or 32 percent), the emotional abuse was ongoing, including name-calling and making severely denigrating comments such as calling her "fat," "ugly," "slut," and "whore."

Twelve women (29 percent) described extreme controlling behaviour that, for some, meant accounting for every minute spent outside the home and, for others, entailed being given a cellular phone so that he could always contact her to find out where she was and what she was doing. Many women were restricted from spending time outside the home with family members or women friends. Nine women (22 percent) described financial abuse such that their partners had literal control over the bank accounts once the women handed their cheques over to their partners. One partner told his wife, who had asked for $5.00, to go down to the "stroll" and make her own money.

Another woman who was out of town at a meeting, to the partner's displeasure, received a phone message from him, claiming that their young child had been hit by a car and was in hospital. She left, only to discover that the entire story was fabricated to force her to return home. Two men, who were not then living with their partners, used to break into their houses at night and wake them up, to their terror. One of the same men would let her know that he'd hidden a gun somewhere inside the house, irrespective of either her fear or the fact that their four young children might come across the firearm.

Five women mentioned that their partners had either threatened to or had actually killed their pets, as a way of controlling or getting even with them. After two of these women left their partners, the men carried out the threats, one by shooting the animals, the other by letting them starve to death.

A large body of literature on the effects of spousal violence on children (Wolfe, Crooks, Lee, McIntyre-Smith, & Jaffe, 2003) describes how children are often either a direct or an indirect target of abusive men. Four women had no children, and in another five cases children had no contact with the perpetrator because they were adults (four), or were living with another parent (five). Of the 32 mothers whose children lived with them, five (16 percent) mentioned that their children were not abused by their fathers. The children of 11 mothers (34 percent) witnessed at least some of the abuse of their mother by their father. The mothers of some of these children have noticed psychological or behavioural problems that they attribute to this. One five-year-old, for example, described as witnessing much of the abuse, commented "I don't care if they kill me; I don't care if I die." Another mother mentioned that her children are starting to swear, and that they are violent when mad at each other, pushing each other down.

Six women (19 percent) described their husbands as emotionally abusing the children, including "raging at a one-and-a-half year old." One described her children as "feeling very controlled by their dad." And another six children (19 percent) were physically hurt by fathers who "punched a five-year-old in the stomach" and "hit my two-year-old son in the head for crying in the car." In the final four cases (13 percent), the children had experienced a mix of physical abuse and were either suspected of having been sexually abused (three), or had been (one child).

Thirty-five of the 41 women (86 percent; the partners of 6 women did not physically hurt them) were physically assaulted by partners at least once in addition to any incidents involving firearms. Six of these 35 women were hurt or held down several times throughout the relationship, describing having been "pushed and hit," "bruised her hand," "held down and threatened to break both her wrists." The remaining 29 women described physical beatings that could have resulted in their deaths. Women described having had knives thrown at them, being thrown into walls or down stairs, having one's head repeatedly beat into the floor, fracturing cheekbones, being kicked in the face or private parts and having bones broken. The partners of ten women choked or strangled them, to the point where two women barely survived the experience. Several women were locked outside in the dead of winter, or were restrained inside the house if their partners were away. One woman was tied to the bed to keep her from leaving. Another woman was burned with cigarettes; one other was slashed across the chest with a knife, requiring 27 stitches.

An issue that remains relatively unacknowledged is the extent to which abusive partners rape their wives (Bergen, 1998). The partners of 22 women (51 percent) forced sex on them. Five women commented that this had occurred once or several times. The other 17 women were raped repeatedly. One woman suffered such severe internal damage that she required surgery and can no longer bear children. Three women commented that they were pressured unwillingly into degrading sexual acts:

> He had an alternative lifestyle. He would suggest things that I was definitely not okay with, but I would just go along with it.

> He sexually assaulted me many, many times. When there's a firearm
> beside the bed, you pretty much know the rules of the household.
> It was an implied threat. Certainly when we're in bed and he's
> within an arm's reach of a gun, you don't need to go further than
> that to know the rules of the game. He'd say, "It was really neat
> when I got that deer last week. Man, I blew his head off!" It wasn't
> like he said, "I'm going to shoot you." You don't need to say that.

Of the 39 women whose partners had an opportunity to stalk them
after they separated, two-thirds (67 percent) described the men as following them, making harassing phone-calls and, in several cases, making a
concerted effort to destroy the women's reputations. One woman was waiting for her husband to be released from jail because of the firearms
incident in which he pointed a shotgun at her. She had fled her hometown
to hide from him, obviously anticipating that he would follow. His threats
to kill her, often subsequently discounted as a joke, signalled that the relationship had become significantly more dangerous.

Without considering the firearms incidents, the partners of 28 women
(68 percent) threatened to kill them. In seven cases, the men threatened to
kill others as well, either children (four) or other family members (three).

> He always used to say that he was going to cut my head off. He had
> a big stack of lime in the field that he'd got in to neutralize the
> alkali. He said, "I could cut your head off and put you in that lime
> pit and no one would ever find you." He threatened to kill my
> father; he threatened to blow up my sister's house.
>
> He stuck the screwdriver in my neck and said, "This is how it
> would feel if I gave you a tracheotomy."
>
> He threatened to pour gasoline over me and light me on fire.

It has been recently acknowledged that a man threatening to commit
suicide also puts women and children at high risk (Campbell, Sharps &
Glass, 2000) but this is not widely known. A relatively high proportion
(17 or 42 percent) of the men in the current study had threatened to both

commit suicide and harm their women partners. In four cases (23 percent of the suicide threats), the husband's threat to commit suicide with a firearm was the most distressing incident. It raised, for the first time, the possibility that the women or others could be shot before he took his own life. In two cases, the man actually pointed the firearm at her. Two suicide threats were in the context of the woman talking about leaving, but not the other two. Two women described the suicide threats as occurring more than once:

> He would pull out the gun and load it and say he was going to kill himself. Usually, he would load them and make threatening remarks, like he was going to commit suicide, and then he would unload them later when things calmed down. After awhile, he didn't even put them away. There were two things that occurred that last night we were together. He pointed the firearm at me, not for very long, only for seconds. I knew when he was pointing it at me that it wasn't really me he was pointing at, but I was also scared for my life for probably two or three seconds. He took this shotgun out of the closet, loaded it, and then pointed it at me, and then he kneeled down and put the barrel in his mouth. I was watching him and then I couldn't look anymore, and then he finally stopped.

Another woman described one traumatic incident that lasted for half an hour, much of which was witnessed by their four-year-old child:

> At one point, we were standing together and the rifle was pointed at me, and he forcibly ejected the clip and said he would blow his head off in front of my face and I would have to try and get my marbles together for the rest of my life. I locked myself and my son in the house.

Nineteen women (46 percent) had firearms pointed at them or actually shot at by their partners. Thankfully, none were injured physically, but the incidents were traumatic. In 12 cases, firearms incidents occurred only once; seven of the 19 women were repeatedly threatened with firearms during the course of their relationships:

He tried to start an argument and I took the clothes out of the dryer and said, "I'm tired of doing nothing. I'm going to start going out too if you're going out." He ran upstairs and loaded the gun. I sat in the living room. I had the laundry basket and he came in with the gun pointed at me and he shot right above my head in the wall. He was going back to the bedroom to reload and I ran after him and let out a scream. I just didn't understand it. There was no reason. I wasn't fooling around. I was just trying to have a life. I always felt he kept the bullet-hole there for a reminder because he filled it over, but never painted. The last time, he said that the beatings helped me understand him. He was so right.

He went downstairs to where he had a gun, got bullets and loaded it, and stood at the end of the bed screaming that I'd ruined his family. He'd kill me first and I'd never leave. I said, "Are you going to shoot me now?" He said, "Yes I am," and he fired it. It was close. I thought he'd shot me. It went through the headboard probably two inches from my head.

The Impact of the Abuse

The women described the impact of the abuse both when they cohabited with their partners and afterwards, if stalked, or while having continued contact because of custody and access issues:

I live in fear every day. I continually suffer from insomnia. Right now, he's under observance by his lawyer, my lawyer, but when the case is over, I'm very afraid. I know him. He can't leave me; he will try to do something against me. Now I have walked out on him — it makes him look, in a small community, pretty bad. So who knows what he'll do to me if he sees me face to face.

Fear, panic attacks, numbness at the time, sheer terror that I was going to die at any time, or he was going to take the children.

He destroyed my feeling of self-worth, self-confidence, even my motivation to survive. There were times I just wanted to die. It was like I can't fight anymore, and then I thought of my kids. My kids were the only thing. I wasn't worth fighting for in my mind. If he wanted to kill me, he could do it any time he wanted. If he wanted to kill my kids, he could do it any time and do you know what he'd get for it? Probably six years.

I still have that fear [the incident when she phoned the police was in 1996]. It's really strange. Two days ago, when I came back to my car, I thought someone was in my car, maybe with a gun. All days I have that fear. All days, when my son doesn't call me one day, I get worried that something happened to him. [So you're still living with it?] Yes.

Afterwards I knew that he could kill me. I'd never had that fear of him before. I knew that he could hurt me, I knew that he could crack a rib, I knew that he could slap me or bruise me, or call me every name in the book, but I didn't know that he had it in him to kill me. I knew that then. [He fired his rifle at her.]

After Thoughts

The stories of these women debunk several of the myths presented in the first section of the paper. A number were highly educated and were professionals, trained as technicians, nurses, chemists and engineers. The majority of the women who had been married previously had not been abused in that relationship and had no understanding about abuse that they could apply to their new partners. With the current high divorce rates, women from past non-abusive relationships may represent a potential focus for prevention education. Whether or not the women had been in an abusive relationship previously or not, most had few warnings that the relationship would become so violent over time. Many left after the first significantly abusive incident; a number were abused only after they had left the relationship, challenging the perception that women typically remain in abusive relationships for years.

It is essential to acknowledge the context of the extremely abusive nature of the partner's abuse. The firearm threats against the women interviewed for this research was only one aspect of the abuse; for some, not even the worst:

> You read in the paper where women have been beaten to death. It really doesn't make a difference whether it's a handgun, a knife, a baseball bat, whatever.

> I don't think the gun is necessarily the problem. The problem is these men walking around like time bombs. I was equally afraid of him when he came home with a hatchet.

Yet, reading the histories of the relationships, in only a few instances could the women have suspected that they were at such risk. The sadistic nature of the violence for virtually all the women respondents is beyond what most of us can imagine. Although the violence was episodic rather than pervasive for a number of the women, the extent to which the men went beyond emotional cruelty and physical abuse, to repeated sexual assaults and threats to kill their partners, remains shocking. However, the abusers must retain the responsibility for the abuse, not the women who were subjected to it.

Despite such profound impacts, these women left their abusive partners and have pulled their lives together in impressive ways. The abuse was a significant part of these women's lives but it does not define them. Beyond the abuse, they were successful mothers, professionals, colleagues. With few exceptions, the interviews seemed like conversations with any friend or neighbour, women living lives similar to any of us.

Their willingness to narrate their stories for the research underlines their strengths. They chose to participate in the hope that their stories would prevent other women from entering abusive relationships or help them to leave earlier. The narratives assign the responsibility for the abuse to the partners who made the choice to behave so reprehensibly. The women's stories affirm that the pathway into abusive relationships is not often predictable. They highlight our commonalities with these resilient women, rather than our differences.

Notes

1 This research was conducted for the Canadian Firearms Centre of the Department of Justice Canada in partnership with the Alberta Council of Women's Shelters, the Edmonton Police Service Spousal Violence Intervention Teams and the Calgary Police Service Domestic Conflict Unit. Thanks to Julie Lovely for her guidance.

CHAPTER THREE

Bound, Bonded and Battered:
Immigrant and Visible Minority Women's Struggle to Cope with Violence

Nayyar Javed in partnership with Nikki Gerrard

The silence on violence against women in the global community was first broken at the United Nations Human Rights Forum in Vienna in 1993. Women from across the globe shared the stories of their struggle in a special tribunal to convince the world community to acknowledge violence against women as a human-rights violation. However, the silence on family violence in the cultural communities of immigrant and visible minority women in Canada has yet to be broken. The story of their struggle to cope has not been heard in their own voice and therefore they are misrepresented in the institutions that are working to protect women from violence. The social exclusion of immigrant and visible minority women has played a significant role in perpetuating their silence.

The exclusion leads them to strengthen the bondedness with their cultural communities, despite the horrific cultural traditions such as honour killing, female genital mutilation and many other violations of women's human rights. Bondedness to culture is a common human experience. However, it often gains salience for immigrant and visible minority women who live in a racist society which, in turn, thwarts their need for belonging and self-validation.

This context is the legacy of colonial discourse (Narayan, 1997) which has historically represented non-white populations as racially inferior

(Fanon, 1963). The assumptions about this supposed inferiority have been used to justify a social treatment of these populations that fosters inequality and social exclusion (Duncan, 2003). They are seen and treated as *other*.

Before I go further, I must locate myself in this work. I am a woman from Pakistan who has lived in the West for over forty years. There is within me the presence of a nagging hesitancy, which has persistently interfered with my writing this chapter. Rationally speaking, this hesitancy contradicts the feminist consciousness I have worked so hard to develop. At the emotional level, however, I am scared of saying what I need to say. This fear is deeply linked to what I have observed in the media, and to the broader social context. As I said before, any episode of family violence in immigrant and visible minority communities is often attributed to culture. Cultural explanations of this violence often ignore its presence in the mainstream Canadian culture. Singling out the cultures of Canadian immigrants is yet another way of reinforcing the superiority of Western culture.

Representing other cultures as inferior is a common practice and not restricted to the media; it also prevails in the academic world. I am very aware of this practice and therefore hesitate to break the silence. I have noticed a similar hesitancy in other feminist scholars who are themselves either immigrants or visible minorities in Canada. This hesitancy is also very much present in feminist scholars of the developing world.

I have experienced some unpleasant encounters as the result of talking about honour killing at international as well as Canadian levels. Feminists of colour in Canada and feminists from developing countries were offended by my position. Their criticism expressed a fear of exposing their cultures to stigma. Despite this criticism, I feel relatively safe with them and value those moments when we can argue frankly with each other without fear of exposing our culture to the persistent scrutiny of these cultures — what Bannerji (1993) calls the "racist gaze."

My hesitancy is grounded in my life experiences. The country of my origin was a former British colony. I grew up in the now-past colonial era. The bitter memories of humiliating experiences were still fresh in people's minds. We had not yet forgotten the impact of the supremacy of western culture and the colonialist perception of our culture. This perception caused a strong reaction, which was a mixture of hostility and a heightened allegiance to the traditional culture of our land. I learned to protect my culture from the "racist gaze" with utmost vigilance. Moving to Canada exposed my cultural heritage to this gaze at different levels.

I used to run groups for battered women in my workplace. Few visible minority and immigrant women would attend, and when they did, their presence invariably evoked the colonial imagery in other participants who were themselves abused by their partner. Yet, they would often make inappropriate comments about the cultures of these visible minority women. I have witnessed similar attitudes of mainstream western women towards other cultures at many international conferences, including the sessions of the UN Commission on the Status of Women. Over the years, I have learned not to react. But in the earlier stages of my involvement in the Canadian women's moment, these experiences were quite shocking. Here is an example:

> I was the Saskatchewan Representative to the National Action Committee on the Status of Women (NAC) in 1990. NAC used to have a lobby session with the Members of Parliament (MPs) in the House of Commons during its Annual General Meeting. In that year's session, I raised a concern about the lack of resources for appropriate services for abused immigrant and refugee women. A female Liberal MP responded by saying that immigrant men need to be "Canadianized" to stop their violence against women. Yet, according to Statistics Canada (2000), male violence against women is as pervasive in Canada as in other countries and, therefore, immigrant men would not learn very much from Canadian men. The MP was either ignorant of this fact or was looking through a racist lens, where men with different skin colour appeared "barbaric" to her and in need of Canadianization to become civilized.

All these experiences return to me as I sort out my thoughts and feelings about violence against immigrant and visible minority women. There is pain, but there is also the inspiration from my sisters who have survived this violence.

Social Exclusion and Bondedness to Cultural Community

This concept of social inclusion and exclusion has recently emerged in the worldwide multicultural discourse. According to Duncan (2003), social inclusion is "a policy promoted in an inclusive society to grant access to everyone to the vehicles of the good life, as it is deemed by the society" (p. 31). Social exclusion, on the other hand, is caused by setting limits on the means to achieve the "good life." The intersection of race, gender and culture (which I illustrate in a case example later in this paper) plays a dominant role in restricting the access of immigrant and visible minority women to the "vehicles of the good life." This, in turn leads to a heightened vulnerability to family violence. In many instances, these women are victimized not only by their partners, but also by male and often female relatives.

Bondedness To Cultural Community

These women face many systemic barriers that hinder their integration into the broader social context. They become dependent on their family and cultural community. This dependence contributes to factors which prevent them from disclosing the violence. Their voices are seldom heard.

Language. The loss of voice is engendered by limiting their access to the means of a "good life." For example, the current language training programs are neither adequate nor gender sensitive. They do not take into consideration women's gendered role, which, for example, includes the provision of childcare, and thus the need for flexible hours for language training classes.

Credentials. The lack of adequate mechanisms for the acceptance of foreign credentials and work experience is a major roadblock for immigrant women trying to find jobs that match their qualifications. Most of them end up working long hours for minimum wage and have no opportunities for advancement (Smith, 2004). They work and yet remain poor (CRIAW, 2002).

Racism. Racism affects all people who are members of a visible minority, but it affects women differently than men. Racism is a categorization of superiority within the human species which places different races in different ranks of value and importance. The white-skinned male (with less pigmentation) of European descent is assumed to be the most superior of all. Scientific legitimacy granted to these assumptions has recently been challenged (Outlaw, 1990). However, erasing the notion of the superiority of white European males from a Western collective consciousness has remained an unmet challenge. The biological legitimacy accorded to race and gender, as categories for ranking human beings, has serious implications for women, who are seen as biologically deficient on both these grounds. This assumed deficit produces and reproduces what Essed (2001) has conceptualized as gendered-racism. Gendered-racism has painful material, social and psychological consequences for racialized women. It pushes them to the margin in all social relations.

Furthermore, "everyday racism" (Essed, 1991) exists in informal social interactions in neighbourhoods and shopping centres. Essed differentiates "everyday racism" from the institutionalized racism found in workplaces, schools, health-care systems, etc. "Everyday racism" includes racial slurs and physical attacks in public and private places. This "everyday racism" isolates visible minority women from society (Ng, 1993). The racist, stereotypic image of these women, which is prevalent in our society, fosters persistent devaluation of their personhood by treating them as inferior in every way. This makes it very hard for them to feel equal to other Canadians. As well, they are aware of how they are perceived. They find themselves being seen and treated as the *others* in contrast to the real citizens of Canada (Said, 1979; Miles, 1989; and Goldberg, 1990).

This otherness is a major source of their vulnerability for family violence. The violence against these women does not get adequate attention from the state, as Canadian public policies do not reflect sensitivity to the issues relating to empowering these women.

In order to grasp what it means to be an immigrant woman, even if the woman has gained the legal status of a citizen, it is important to explore why some women are seen as immigrant and other women are not. Some women who do not appear to be visible minorities are seldom described as immigrant. Conversely, there are many *other* women who may have lived in Canada as citizens for decades, yet in the public eye they have remained as "immigrant women" because of their visible minority status. Ironically, their Canadian-born daughters and even granddaughters are also seen and treated as immigrant. This difference in perception cannot be described in any other way than as a resistance to granting real, not just legal, citizenship to all Canadians (Ng, 1993).

The category known as "visible minority" creates huge barriers to their feeling as if they belong in Canadian society. In Participatory Action Research, conducted by the Saskatoon chapter of Immigrant Women of Saskatchewan (IWS) on the Health Determinants of Immigrant Women, the participants cited the lack of social space for feeling like they belong in Canada (i.e., social exclusion) as a major negative health determinant in their lives (Javed, 2002; also see Galabuzi, 2004 and Labonte, 2004 for further discussions of social exclusion and health determinants). The term "visible minority" has become a much resisted social identity (Carty & Brand, 1998) for non-white Canadians because it is often used to determine an exclusionary social relation and therefore serves the politics of exclusion (Minh-Ha, 1993; Duncan, 2003).

Consequences

There are painful psychological consequences of this social exclusion.

"Twoness." The "twoness" of self, identified by Dubois (1998), plays a major role in this regard. Twoness is a deep division within oneself that makes one feel simultaneously a citizen and an alien. This division leads to a sense of "dislocated self" (Minh-Ha, 1993), which is a profound sense of feeling out of place within one's own body. The reconciliation of this division becomes difficult because of constant reminders of otherness from the "real" citizens (Miles, 1989). In the IWS research, participants revealed that twoness causes a deep sense of alienation in immigrant and visible minority women (Javed, 2002).

Gender differences in social identity. Over the years, I have observed gender differences in the way racialized women and men resist the social identity which has been imposed on them. This difference seems to be linked to gender roles and cultural expectations. For example, the masculine identity defined by racialized men's cultures gives them a sense of entitlement to social privileges. On the contrary, the racialized social identity imposed on them in Canada takes those privileges away from them. They feel marginalized in a broader social context, which is not a familiar experience for men who have immigrated to Canada. They turn to the cultural traditions that legitimize women's subordination to return to the men a sense of power and control. On the other hand, women are expected to accept a subordinate position to compensate for the marginality men experience in the broader social context (DasGupta, 1994a and b). Home and cultural community often become the site for men to draw the support for feeling powerful, and for women to offer this support to men at the cost of women's own needs. This is a dangerous situation for these women, who simply cannot make up for the loss of power men experience outside their home and cultural community, and they are seen as failures.

This perceived failure of women to support men through the loss of their presumed privileges and entitlements is not without consequences. Women are punished by family and the cultural community in all sorts of ways, including abandonment. Immigrant and visible minority women are afraid of this punishment. They hesitate to talk about the violence in their lives, not only to protect themselves from the punishment by their family and cultural communities, but also to protect their whole culture from the ensuing stigma. Violence against women in ethnic communities is often portrayed in the mainstream media as a cultural problem.

Pride in their culture and the fear of abandonment by the cultural community lead racialized women into making this choice of silence when they experience violence. This choice is often made to protect their culture and men from the "racist gaze" (Bannerji, 1993). The stereotypic images society has of these women does not allow those in mainstream society who have not interrogated their own racism to go beyond these images and see the high degree of resilience these women have developed to cope with the intersection of race, gender and culture which they are trapped in. The responsibility of protecting the reputation of their culture and men takes an enormous emotional toll and poses a risk to their safety. Failing to fulfil, this responsibility, however, is equally risky. They are often very well aware of this risk. They know the consequences of betraying their culture by stepping out of its bounds, which demand submission to male supremacy. Families ensure compliance to the rules of their respective cultures.

Examples Of Bondedness to Cultural Community and Consequences

I met a young woman in a conference in Winnipeg in 1993. She looked lost and sad. I was drawn to her. She shared her story. She told me she got romantically involved with a young man of a different racial background, which according to her family's cultural background was equivalent to a crime. She had violated the honour of her family and, therefore, could have been killed. Her family decided to spare her life and punish her a bit more mildly. She was ostracized. The young woman was quite attached to her mother. The separation from her mother was putting a huge emotional strain on her. She expressed a deep sorrow and would have done anything to make some connection with her mother. However, she knew that it was not possible because her family was not willing to be the target of rejection and shame by its cultural community.

I also met a young woman in Toronto who left an extremely abusive husband. She was asked by her cultural community to stay away from them, as she would corrupt other women. This woman was a qualified and experienced lawyer in her country of origin, but restrictions on the acceptance of foreign credentials prevented her from practising law. She was doing a menial job to support herself while getting training as a massage therapist.

It is important to point out that these examples illustrate other consequences of social exclusion. First, the marginalization of racialized women, practised by mainstream society, is reproduced within their own cultural communities. Secondly, the gender differences related to social exclusion demonstrate that men experience exclusion from *outside* their cultural communities while women experience exclusion, doubly, from both *outside and inside* their cultural communities. The exclusion from mainstream society for racialized women is not only as racialized individuals but also as women.

The Silence

Thus far I have discussed social exclusion: how immigrant and visible minority women become bonded to their cultural community and some of the resultant consequences. When violence occurs in these women's relationships, it is met with silence. How and why this silence occurs is discussed below.

Nowhere to Go

A recent study by the Canadian Council on Social Development (CCSD) entitled *Nowhere to Go* (Smith, 2004) explores violence against immigrant and visible minority women. This research is the first attempt in Canadian history to map out the extent of male violence in ethnic cultural communities. Its title, *Nowhere to Go*, captures the reality of the women within the communities, including the lack of culturally sensitive services and the pervasiveness of poverty. It also extensively reflects on the role of the state in imposing silence on the issue of male violence in ethnic communities.

The CCSD's report (Smith, 2004) acknowledges a vast cultural and linguistic diversity among immigrant women, along with identifying their shared reality of having "nowhere to go." They are isolated as they face huge structural barriers in being accepted by society. They have lost their voice, and experience a profound sense of powerlessness since they do not have opportunities to learn English or French. They lost their social support systems when they moved to Canada. They can turn to their ethnic communities for support, but if they speak out about violence in their home they find themselves abandoned. They are without money because they cannot find jobs. Neither their credentials nor their work experience is recognized. When they turn to the judicial system, they find it unresponsive. They keep their mouths shut because "there is already a lot of discrimination against our community. There is domestic violence in our community, but we don't talk about it because we don't want to reinforce the prejudice. It can feed into the stereotypes. People already think, 'You come from a violent place ...'" (Smith, 2004, p. 4).

The issue of needing to protect culture from stigma emerged as a significant cause of silencing women as well. Structural barriers, such as the lack of adequate language training programs and the rejection of foreign credentials and work experience, were identified as major roadblocks to social integration. Racial prejudice in society, an unresponsive judicial system and lack of public services for battered women were other major problems.

The complexity of the experiences of abused immigrant and visible minority women may seem overwhelming. Anybody who works with these women can attest to this. It is time to start dealing with violence in their lives. Breaking the silence is the first step in the process, but there is the fear of stigmatizing cultures. Exposing men to a racist justice system and over-coming the structural barriers that prevent women from gaining economic independence. Women hesitate because they are afraid.

Ms. T.

The following is an example of a client I have seen in my practice, and it provides an understanding of the way gender, race and culture intersect with each other in the lives of immigrant and visible minority women. Coping with this intersection is a struggle.

I saw Ms. T. for five sessions. She cancelled the sixth session for fear of her husband finding out that she was in therapy. Initially, she came to see me about the distress she was experiencing because her only son, 30 years old, had become terminally ill. Ms. T. and her family had gone through a civil war in their country of origin, prior to moving to Canada. She was a professional in that country, quite well off and living in a nice home. At the time of her therapy, she was a part-time dishwasher in a restaurant here in Saskatoon. She lived with her husband in a one-bedroom basement apartment. Her husband had been emotionally abusive from the very beginning of their 30 years of marriage. He started to hit her after they came to Canada.

She phoned from her workplace to tell me she was stopping the therapy. She said she had never told anybody about being hit by her husband. One reason for her silence was that she felt isolated because of the language barrier and not knowing anybody other than the people in her own community. She said she would never tell them about the abuse as they would not believe her and might see her as a "westernized" woman. She remained silent to protect her husband from the police. She thought if the police found out, he might be arrested and treated badly, because that is what they do to a "foreigner." She expressed fear of being deported, since she had come to Canada as a dependent of her husband. And she remained silent because she was working part-time at minimum wage, which would hardly enable her to support herself.

Ms. T. expressed profound disappointment about Canada's rejection of her professional degree and experience and did not ever want to go on social assistance. She was supporting her mother who was still living in her "home" country; her husband did not know about the little bit of money she would occasionally send to her mother.

Ms. T.'s situation captures some of the features of the painful reality of immigrant and visible minority women struggling with the intersections of race, gender, and culture. It also demonstrates the role that economic oppression plays in maintaining and even enforcing their silence. These intersections create layers of oppression. Knowledge of realities such as this helps in understanding why these women are reluctant to break the silence about their pain.

Breaking the Silence

The fear of breaking the silence is embedded in a complex configuration of circumstances, which I have discussed above. There are instances of abandonment of women by their family and cultural community. For example, a woman who immigrated from one of the South Asian countries finally decided to end a thirty-year marriage. She and her ex-husband were living in a smaller community in Canada. This woman was ostracized by her cultural community and relatives who were still living in her country of origin. Her brothers told her never to return. This is not an exceptional situation. There is a multitude of similar examples. Women are afraid of disclosing family secrets. They may become depressed or take their lives rather than lose the support of their cultural community or family, here in Canada or back home.

Immigrant and visible minority women are not a homogenous group. They have diverse cultural, class, religious and linguistic backgrounds. Their only commonality is social exclusion and an imposed marginalized identity and isolation. Their racial backgrounds isolate them. This isolation causes silence about violence in their lives. The Canadian state and the women's cultural community are complicit in perpetuating this silence.

Policy Formation

At the state level, transformation of the process of policy formation is critical in making the social change required for finding the solution to the social exclusion of immigrant and visible minority women, especially those who are underprivileged within these groups. The transformation requires a deliberate effort by government to include the voices of these women. Unfortunately, cutbacks in funding that we have seen in the past decade have seriously eroded the level of participation of all grass-root women in the process of policy formation. The underprivileged immigrant and visible minority women have been pushed further aside from this process. Consequently, the programs for language training and the initiatives for acceptance of foreign credentials and access to meaningful employment have been negatively affected.

On another front, in Saskatchewan, the government has recently taken more control over immigration policy in order to encourage more immigrants to move to and stay in Saskatchewan. We now have a settlement policy within the province. Gender issues such as child care and capacity building of women's organizations, which advocate for women's specific need for equality, have not yet been considered important in the initial stages of policy formation.

Globally, the impact of the September 11 terrorist attacks has added new policy challenges. September 11 has resulted in further strengthening some of the barriers that prevent immigrant and visible minority women's access to social inclusion (Mohammed, 2004). For example, the enforcement of security legislation and racial profiling has restricted the mobility of Muslim women and all other racialized women who look like Muslim women. This has created mistrust in the immigrant and visible minority communities. Ironically, the heightened protection of these women, by their ethnic communities, has resulted in less freedom for them.

The Canadian Research Institute for the Advancement of Women (CRIAW) and the National Organization of Immigrant and Visible Minority Women (NOIVMW) have recently undertaken a research project to explore the impact of September 11 on the lives of Muslim women. The findings of this research show a broad range of obstacles, which are eroding the social inclusion of not only Muslim women but also other racialized women. The various post-September 11 security measures (e.g. the proposal to demand security cards, greater access to phone-tapping, sharing of information with other countries, etc.) have increased the need for special measures to ensure the security of immigrant and visible minority women not only from family violence, but also from other forms of violence, including violence in public and workplaces. The need for this security clearly reflects challenges for public policy.

Policy Analysis

The Canadian government has attempted to use the Gender-Based Analysis (GBA) (CRIAW, 2004), in regards to public policy. The GBA identifies the gender impact of a given policy. For instance, it points out how a policy advances or erodes women's equality in society. Unfortunately, the GBA has not been applied in all areas of public policy and does not take into account the intersection of gender and race.

More recently, feminists of colour have proposed an alternative analysis, namely the Integrated Feminist Analysis (IFA) (CRIAW, 2004), in order to take the intersections of gender, race and other marginalized identities of women into account in the formation of public policy. An across-the-board IFA of the policies of the Saskatchewan government may help to open the door for immigrant and visible minority women to gain access to social inclusion, and break the silence about all forms of violence, including racial violence. For instance, an IFA of employment policies may identify barriers foreign-trained professional women face in finding jobs in their own professions. This may provide them with economic independence, thereby allowing them more freedom to speak out about the violence in their relationships.

Research

The feminist research community needs to open its eyes to the violence immigrant and visible minority women experience in Canada. Both research by and solidarity from the mainstream feminist community are critical for the empowerment of women whose vulnerability to violence, as I have demonstrated in this paper, is linked to their gender, racial and cultural identities.

Limitations of This Chapter and Final Words

This chapter has left out many issues that also need attention. For example, my focus on the "ethnic community" has excluded a discussion of family violence in mixed-race marriages, especially the cases of "mail-order brides" and the marriages between immigrant women and white Canadian men. In my practice, I have come across horrific stories in such situations. I also did not talk about the impact of many problematic practices, such as forced marriages or family coercion for early marriages, on the lives of young women. In fact, the issues of the "girl-child," which is so important in discussing family violence in ethnic communities, was not even mentioned in this chapter. No one chapter or even one book can cover the multiple dimensions of family violence in the lives of immigrant and visible minority women, because the issue is so complex.

I wrote this chapter not as an expert, but as someone who has had the honour of listening to the stories of many wonderful women. No one but the survivors of the violence must claim expertise. Their resilience has been an incredible source of inspiration in my life.

Notes:

1   Bondedness to culture, according to Narayan (1997), is a relationship an individual has with her or his culture or ethnicity. Identification of self with culture constitutes the core of this relationship; because of this, an individual develops a profound sense of allegiance to their culture.

2   Racialized refers to a social construct based on a racist ideology and represents people in a hierarchical way with white people at the top and people of colour at the bottom. An obvious result is the "inferiorization" of people of colour.

CHAPTER FOUR

Understanding Theories and their Links to Intervention Strategies

Carmen Gill

Understanding Domestic Violence

Domestic violence is not a new phenomenon, but it is relatively recently that the issue has been recognized as a major social problem and as a crime (Johnson, 1996). To understand how domestic violence, and especially women abused by intimate partners, became a major issue in Canadian society, it is necessary to look broadly at it in a socio-historic continuum. Laws in place today in Canada are a result of denunciation from various groups and members of the feminist movement. Historically, domestic violence has been viewed as a *normal* situation in the family, supported by a *normal* century-old legacy suggesting that women are deserving victims: "The law historically sanctioned the abuse of women within marriage as an aspect of a husband's ownership of his wife and his right to chastise her" (Status of Women Canada, 2002, p. 2). Men were given great latitude to correct any behaviour that they considered inappropriate for their partners. The notion that a woman was to be corrected by her husband is thus strongly rooted in our society and such behaviour has long been seen as socially tolerable. It is easy to find historical examples of normalization of violence and abuse in the context of Canadian families. So when it comes to understanding domestic violence, we have to keep in mind that historical background influences contemporary comprehension of the issue and affects debates about who the victims are, as well as giving explanations for domestic violence.

Hence, as a starting point to understanding the issue, we must see that the development of explanations for domestic violence is interconnected with, and influenced by, the deconstruction of women and children as property of husband and father (Backhouse, 1991). Our understanding of domestic violence progressed once it was seen as an issue of victimization of both children and adults (Barnett, Miller-Perrin & Perrin, 1997).

Approaching Domestic Violence

In Canada, before the 1970s, violence was "officially" rare, as very few incidents were reported. When males were convicted, they were generally depicted as mentally ill, while female victims were perceived as unstable, provocative, or masochistic. Domestic violence was viewed as a *private* matter that was to be treated as a *private* family problem. Consequently, the solution to family problems was to come from inside the family. Criminal-justice intervention was not considered a social priority, because domestic violence did not threaten the public order. What has been emphasized since the seventies is the public intervention in domestic violence issues, through criminalization (Johnson, 2000a), the recognition of, and inter-vention with, the victims, and different explanations of the cause of violence. Domestic violence is now viewed as a gender, social, and systemic problem that needs to be addressed publicly, through state intervention. MacLeod (1980) conducted the first study that provided an estimate of the preva-lence of wife battering in Canada, using a sample of women residing in transition houses across the country. She concluded that "... every year, one in ten Canadian women who are married or in relationship with a live-in lover are battered" (1980, p. 1). Since then, communities and researchers have been working together to find solutions to family violence (Stirling, Cameron, Nason-Clark & Miedema, 2004; Tutty & Goard, 2002).

Researchers have attempted to explain causal factors at play in domes-tic violence. Explanations are interconnected with intervention strategies designed to eradicate domestic violence in Canada. In this chapter, we will look at some of those studies that have provided understanding of the issue by exploring diverse theoretical explanations developed from a Canadian viewpoint. The lens here will be primarily on Canadian research that uses various approaches to understand domestic violence. Our objective in this discussion is to connect theoretical explanations to intervention strategies, and to argue that a clear understanding of the causes of domestic violence can lead to an effective intervention strategy and help communities to develop more effective responses to violence (Jasinski, 2001). Considering that a clear understanding of the causes of domestic violence can lead to an effective intervention strategy, we are thus using a dialectical process by which theoretical explanations are connected to intervention strategies.

Defining Domestic Violence

Different terms are used in the literature to speak about violence in the family. Depending on the researcher's standpoint, the targeted actors in a study can be the abusers, the victims, or the witnesses. The term selected will convey a certain understanding of the issue. For instance, what distinction can be made between *conjugal violence, domestic violence, family violence,* and *violence against women*? Mann (2000) provides a substantive discussion on terminology used in the literature, explaining that the term *violence against women* is grounded in a feminist perspective and the term *family violence* reflects a sociological and helping-professional perspective. As Mann notes, some researchers suggest that these two terms refer in some ways to different issues within the spectrum of abuse. She qualifies the distinction made between the two as "inflammatory rhetoric" (p. 13) that forces the reader to revise his/her understanding of the issue. We agree with Mann that rhetorical debates do not provide answers to the causes of abuse or solutions to eliminate violence, but they do demonstrate the diversity of views and interpretations of abuse phenomena. It is important to recognize the diversity in labelling and defining the issue, in order to delimit the parameters used to select specific theoretical explanations.

While reading the literature, I found variation in terminology. *Family violence* is a designation encompassing violence against any member in the family-setting (child, teen, woman, man, elder). Duffy and Momirov (1997) use this term but recognize the gendered nature of family violence. Thus, for many researchers (Gelles, 1997), *family violence* has a larger implication than *conjugal* or *domestic* violence, *violence against women*, or *woman abuse*. In French, use of the term *conjugal violence* (Larouche, 1987) is related to violence between intimate partners, similar to the term *domestic violence* in English. Yet, other researchers have used the same term to emphasize a broader definition, inclusive of both genders. For instance, Buzawa & Buzawa (2002) use the term *domestic violence* as a gender neutral one, suggesting that violence is a problem for both genders.

The use of the term *violence against women*, on the other hand, clearly states that violence is not gender-neutral and that women are more at risk of violence; it encompasses all types of violence towards them. It represents "unique aspects of the wider social problem of violence ..." (Johnson, 1996, p. xx). Martin (1996) states that all violence against women is characterized by "an abuse of power perpetrated by one or many men in a society where gender-based relations are unequal and often synonymous with domination" (free translation). The use of the term *woman abuse* (DeKeseredy & MacLeod, 1997; Miedema & Nason-Clark, 2004; Tutty & Goard, 2002) clearly states that, although violence can affect every member of the family, women are more often at risk in their intimate relationship: "For example, twice as many women as men are beaten, five times as many choked, and almost twice as many have a gun or knife against them" (Status of Women, 2002, p. 12).

I have refined the term *domestic violence* by using the postulate Tutty & Goard (2002) made about women abused by intimate partners. Recognizing that husband abuse remains relatively rare, they remind us that the abuse of women still occurs much more frequently than the opposite. Along with sexual assault, violence between intimate partners "... is one of the two forms of violence against women that has received the most theoretical development...." (Jasinski, 2001, p. 5). From this standpoint, focusing on women as victims of violence by their intimate partner will explain our criteria for selecting specific studies presented.

In this chapter, I will discuss theoretical perspectives on women abused by their intimate partner. Using mostly Canadian literature, I want firstly to introduce two umbrellas of explanations: micro/individual and macro/societal. Secondly, among micro/individual explanations, I distinguish between social learning theory, psychopathological theory, and situational, evolutionary, and sex-role theories. Thirdly, I present macro/societal explanations, such as resource, lifestyle/routine activities, social control and feminist theory. This overview of theoretical explanations will be connected to intervention strategies in order to highlight how theoretical understandings are crucial in orienting the response that community, professionals, and society will give to the issue. Finally, I conclude by arguing that theoretical explanations determine the type of intervention strategies that one will put in place.

A Plethora of Explanations

Theoretical explanations for the abuse of women by their intimate partners have been developed in an attempt to respond to the question: what causes battering? This question remains of interest, even with the impressive number of studies conducted on woman abuse, because there is still no definitive scientific evidence describing factors most strongly correlated with intimate violence. On the intervention side, women can now receive services while in a violent situation; mandatory policies have been put in place and abusive men are receiving treatment. Still, the problem is not neutralized and does not seem to go away.

The development of theoretical perspectives on women abused by their intimate partners has contributed to demystification of persistent myths about why women stay with their abusers for so long when the situation is so bad. Myths are used in a general perspective, as explanations of violence between intimate partners, but can lead to misunderstanding of the issue. Theoretical explanations are helpful in describing contextual elements, in order to accurately understand the dynamics at play between intimate partners and to grasp some causes of partner abuse. There are competing explanations ranging from individual problems and family factors to the recognition of societal and systemic dimensions. There are diverse typologies that have systematized these different explanations.

Gelles & Strauss (1979) developed the first typology of explanations which identifies 15 theories organized into three main categories: intra-individual theory, social psychological theory, and socio-cultural theory. This typology was revised by Johnson (1996), who distinguished individual-level explanations and societal-level explanations. Barnett, Miller-Perrin & Perrin (1997) speak instead of micro- and macro-oriented theories.

Following the micro/macro categorization, Jasinski (2001) further expands the review of theoretical perspectives by addressing multi-dimensional explanations and arguing that a good explanation of violence against women might address both social and individual factors. Chamberland (2003) offers an interesting typology by dividing the macro explanations into three subcategories: evolutionary theory, sociological perspectives, and systemic explanations. Some typologies make the distinction between individual approaches, which emphasize the issue as a psychopathological perspective and are oriented toward individual psychology, describing characteristics of abusers and victims. Others make the distinction between explanations focusing on violence by intimate partners as an internal issue inherent to the family, or influenced and caused by social factors and the environment. What is important to remember is that there are diverse ways of delimiting theoretical perspectives and that typologies are used by researchers to frame a conceptual approach to abuse issues.

The typology I present in this chapter will follow the insights of Johnson (1996) and Jasinski (2001) and focus on two mainstream theoretical frameworks: micro/individual and macro/societal-level explanations. Under the micro/individual level explanations, the emphasis is on psychological and individual characteristics of the abuser and the victim, as well as interpersonal dynamics and situational factors such as alcohol, conflict, or stress. This level focuses on learning explanations and the socialization process and does not include social and cultural factors.

Macro/societal-level explanations include an understanding of the larger social systems and institutions that may have an impact on women abused by their intimate partners. Violence is viewed in an extensive context, emphasizing the connection between social conditions and women abused by their intimate partners. The focus is, for instance, on rates of victimization, the degree of acceptance of violence in society, resources available to abusers and victims, and the distribution of power between men and women. The theoretical explanations presented in the table below summarize the different perspectives that are included in our discussion. It illustrates how the two major umbrellas of explanations relate to intervention strategies.

Table 1: Mainstream Theoretical Frameworks on Women Abused by Their Intimate Partners

Theoretical approach	Micro/Individual-Level Explanations	Macro/Societal-Level Explanations	Theoretical approach
	Characteristics of individuals that are violent	Structural factors leading intimate partners to violence	
Psychopathological >	Abusers are disturbed by mental illness, personality disorder. Psychological traits: measured by personality tests.	Personal lifestyle can influence usage of violence. Degree of acceptance of violence determined by cultural beliefs, marital status as well as age, employment and income.	< Lifestyle/routine
Social learning >	Exposure and imitation are determinants in violent behaviour. Violence is learned through socialization, mostly family and schools.	Norms in place give more power and a better status to men. Violence is a resource to insure that the norms are respected.	< Resource
Sex roles >	Men and women are learning appropriate masculine and feminine roles. Violence is seen as a masculine behaviour. Power and control are considered masculine characteristics.	Cost/benefit explanation of violence. Men are violent because reward is greater then punishment.	< Social control
Situational >	Relates to the interaction between individuals. Stress is a main factor explaining violence. Drug and alcolhol abuse are also factors explaining violence.	Male domination over women is supported by patriarchy and societal institutions. A major factor enabling violence is that social structures are historically male-dominated.	< Feminist

The purpose of this typology is to distinguish approaches and intervention-related strategies; it is not intended to be exhaustive of all approaches and intervention strategies. Furthermore, more than one of these theories may be applicable to any given case (Caplan, personal communication, 2005). I have to keep in mind that explaining women abused by their intimate partners can sometimes require a multidimensional understanding and lead to diverse interventions (Chamberland, 2003). Following this logic, I agree with the argument made by Jasinski (2001, p. 15) that a good explanation "... might contain both social factors (such as race, class, gender, and culture) and individual characteristics or characteristics of the relationship (e.g., social support, relationship dynamics, alcohol or drug use, and personality characteristics)." The boundaries I trace are working ones for the purpose of the discussion.

Micro/Individual Level Explanations

The thesis of micro/individual explanations is that some individual family members are violent. At this level, researchers and practitioners focus on individuals that are violent or are becoming violent. How can this be explained and what resources have to be put in place to address the problem? Individual-level explanations identify characteristics of individuals who are violent in order to provide the best remedy to help them. Under the micro/individual level explanations I discuss four theoretical perspectives: psychopathological, social learning, sex roles and situational theories.

Psychopathological Theory

According to this theory, the first reaction most people have when hearing about situations of violence between intimate partners is to think that the abuser might be insane or mentally disturbed. Common sense and societal myths make us believe that there is a distortion in the abuser's mind. Early research on violence between intimate partners, prior to 1970, linked the causes of violence to psychopathological problems. Research was mainly conducted on prisoners convicted for the most aggressive assaults: raping women, killing wives, etc. The psychopathological perspective has been used to explain mass violence and child abuse (Kempe, 1962) and to understand why men are abusive. This approach suggests that individuals possess some personality disorder or mental illness that prevents them from experiencing normal inhibitions about the use of violence. It includes personality traits such as low self-esteem of the perpetrator, the need to control and have power over others because of a lack of power in other aspects of their lives, etc. Essentially, it views violent behaviour as deviance from the norm. The problem with this perspective is that it is not clear "... which abnormal personality traits are associated with violence, as well as the circularity of using acts of violence as indicators of mental illness" (Gelles & Strauss, 1979, p. 561). This theory, however, has been used to understand the psychological profile of batterers (Dutton & Golant, 1995). Dutton, a Canadian leader on abusers' psychology, suggests that abusers are not a homogenous group, so there are diverse psychological profiles. Consequently, it is impossible to argue with certainty that a specific profile will inevitably result in aggressive behaviour. The psychopathological approach is also concerned with explaining the personalities of women who stay in violent situations (Pagelow, 1992). I feel we have to be very cautious about blaming women who stay in violent relationship because, as Caplan and Caplan (1999) write, "they do NOT stay because they enjoy the suffering.... Assuming that women are masochistic prevents us from exploring and understanding the real reasons they stay...."(p. 50).

Social Learning Theories

This theory posits that individuals are socialized to use violence. Violence is a learned experience that can be transferred through the family, culture and the media. In this perspective, individuals learn to become abusers through repetitive experiences that show violence as a normal and successful response to difficulties (Bandura, 1971). Bandura has described a process called "modelling" which suggests that people learn through exposure and imitation. Family, in this perspective, is the site of exposure to violence and provides an intense learning environment. Violence is viewed as a problem-solving strategy between individuals. In particular, individuals who experience or witness violence in their family of origin learn that violence is an appropriate tactic for getting what they want. The family becomes the training ground for violence, and aggressive behaviour is a means to obtaining rewards. Some researchers have suggested that violence is learned in the context of socialization in the family and that it is an intergenerational transmission process (O'Leary, 1993). O'Leary (1993, p. 10) suggests that "... across diverse samples, there is no consistently high correlation of child and spouse abuse, but as the level of violence in the family of origin increases, spouse abuse is much more likely."

Studying youth violence, Tremblay (2000) has conducted longitudinal studies of samples of children from infancy to adulthood and his results suggest that children are in their most aggressive phase at the age of three. These results led him to conclude "... that the preschool years are the best window of opportunity to prevent the development of cases of chronic physical aggression" (p. 19). Through his observations of children, Tremblay also found that "... failure to teach children to regulate violent behaviour during the early years leads to poverty much more clearly than poverty leads to violence" (p. 23). The Canadian Council on Social Development and Family Service Canada (2003, p. 3) state that "... exposure to and participation in violence puts children at risk." The role of parents is to help their children deal with violence if they are unable to prevent the exposure, especially media exposure.

In a social learning perspective, exposure to violence is a key element in explaining aggressive behaviour. The media influences individual behaviour and can contribute to violent responses within families.

Research on the influence of the media attempts to understand how the degree of exposure to violence can increase the risks of children adopting certain behaviours. The National Clearinghouse of Family Violence (1993) has produced a report looking at the effect of media on individuals and at the correlation between media violence and aggressive behaviour. One recent Canadian intervention study found that the introduction of television into a community can influence the verbal and physical expressions of violence among children (Macbeth-Williams, 1986).

Social learning theory has provided explanations to help us understand why individuals are violent. On the other hand, using the operant conditioning model, Walker (1984) developed the learned-helplessness perspective to explain why women stay in abusive relationships. In her work on battered women, she found that women find it difficult to leave an abusive relationship because they are trapped in the cycle of violence in which the honeymoon stage follows violent episodes and reinforces their desire to stay with the abuser (Walker, 1984). According to Bowker (1993), the learned-helplessness concept as presented by Walker portrays women as passive rather than as individuals actively seeking help. Comack (1993), however, argued that some women are not trapped in this pattern of violence and are in fact breaking the cycle. Critics of the learned-helplessness concept make the distinction between psychological perspectives and societal explanations for violence between intimate partners. In contrast, evidence suggests that what, on the surface, may appear as helplessness is really an attempt to find some strategy that is effective.

Sex Role Theory

The sex role theory is a social learning perspective that suggests that men and women learn "gendered" behaviour through the process of socialization. Gender-based behaviour often legitimizes aggressive behaviour towards women. Males and females first learn gendered stereotypes that are determined by social institutions; then stereotypes encourage gendered behaviour. An illustration of this perspective can be found in the history of the legal response to violence. Sheeny (1999) reminds us that legislation in Canada up until the 1980s emphasized sex role differences by recognizing distinct rights of men and women. Consequently, the legislation supported gender distinction and female inferiority was seen as legally appropriate. Therefore, sex role theory has long been a dominant perspective used to explain men's and women's roles in society.

According to sex role theory, society values masculine qualities like toughness, control, and sexual power, which can be used to reinforce sexual violence and wife-battering. Furthermore, women's main role is to protect her children and assume responsibility for the quality of the marital relationship. Because men and women are raised in different ways, it is seen as acceptable for men to be more aggressive then women from this perspective.

A study of the military response to woman abuse conducted by Harrison (2000; 2004) is a good example of the exacerbation of the sex role differences. Her study shows how imprinted gender differences lead to the organization of social relationships in the military. Of course, the military community has its own organizational structure, but this particular community "... takes for granted the naturalness of the patriarchal notion of a masculine-feminine polarity, or the idea that men and women are fundamentally different" (Harrison, 2004, p. 175). In the military, men are challenged to become real men by showing they are not women. Understanding violence between intimate partners through sex role theory puts the focus on the way men and women are raised, and suggests that deconstruction of those roles is essential to eliminate violence.

Situational Theories

Situational theories, also known as "stress and coping theory" (Gelles, 1997) or "caregiver stress theory" (Podnieks, 1988, in Duffy & Momirov, 1997), explain violence in regard to specific factors. The first factor identified as leading to aggressive behaviour is stress. Family is the site of conflict and stress, and people cope differently with particular events. Raising children, conception of male-female roles, loss of employment, or difficulties in the workplace are a few examples that illustrate stressful situations. In this perspective, violence occurs as a result of crisis situations and responses to the stress and frustration individuals are experiencing. Those crisis situations are associated with poverty, unemployment, and financial and work responsibilities (Johnson, 1996). Confronted with conflicts, an individual may experience low self-esteem, loss of control and lack of power, the responses to which are sometimes expressed through violence towards the partner. The risk of becoming violent with a partner is lower if individuals receive support from friends and family (DeKeseredy & MacLeod, 1997).

Another situational factor identified by the literature is the abuse of alcohol and drugs (National Clearinghouse on Family Violence (2000, p. 10–11): "... fathers who drank to excess were six times as likely to use violence against their own children compared to those who were not heavy drinkers." Explaining violence between intimate partners as the result of the abuse of alcohol has generated controversies in the analysis of causes of violence and in the appropriateness of intervention strategies. The question remains open regarding whether or not alcohol is a direct cause of violence. Flanzer (1993) is convinced that alcohol or other drug (AOD) intake, abuse, and dependency are key causative agents of violence in the family. Other researchers refuse to claim that alcoholism causes family violence, but suggest that the abuser can use it to excuse his aggressive behaviour (Jasinski, 2001). However, the correlation between violence and alcohol is strong enough to take this observation into consideration in regards to intervention with some batterers. As shown in the 1993 National Violence Against Women Survey: "Women were at six times the risk of being assaulted by partners who frequently consumed five or more drinks at one time, compared to partners who never drank" (Rodgers, 1994; in DeKeseredy & Macleod, 1997, p. 35).

Macro/Societal-level Explanations

Instead of focusing on the characteristics of individuals who are violent, macro/societal-level explanations emphasize the structural factors that lead intimate partners to violence. Questions discussed in macro-level explanations include: how do culture and social institutions support or encourage violence between intimate partners, and how are economic, gender and/or social inequalities key dimensions leading to violence between intimate partners? There are several perspectives developed around the socio-cultural determinants that are seen as direct causes of violence, including four particular theories: lifestyle routine activities, resource theory, exchange/ social control, and feminist theory.

Lifestyle/Routine Activities Theory

According to this theory, exposure to violence increases with high-risk situations involving factors such as income level, marital status, age, and employment status. Research from this perspective focuses on causes of victimization and explanation of crime. By establishing who is more likely to be victimized it is possible to find solutions to violence. This perspective focuses on the access to women by motivated abusers, and comprises research on university and college women who are sexually assaulted. Women who are young, single and have low incomes are at a higher risk of suffering from violence because of their lifestyle. The risk of assault is further increased when there are real or perceived opportunities for access, such as a lack of protection from a spouse or family member. According to Schwartz and Pitts (1995), two lifestyle factors which can increase the likelihood of women being assaulted are: 1) drinking to the point that a woman cannot resist a man; and 2) attending parties where there are potential abusers. Cohen and Felson (1979) argued that the focus has to be on the constant motivation to commit crime. Some lifestyles or routine activities render people more vulnerable to assault in their everyday lives (Van Brunschot, 2000). Three key lifestyle/routine activities have been found to be risk factors: 1) the access to suitable targets; 2) the lack of capable guardians; and 3) the presence of motivated offenders. Those elements are used to explain criminal activities but they are problematic when it comes to understanding violence between intimate partners. As pointed out by Johnson (2000b), lifestyle/routine activities can be an efficient rationale to understanding abuse by strangers or random abuse, but is unable to explain violence between intimate partners:

> Clearly, a different perspective is necessary to explain the causes of wife assault and dating violence, since the greatest risk factor, according to lifestyle/routine activities, is to be married, dating, or living with a man (p. 126).

In sum, the lifestyle/routine activities perspective highlights some causes of woman abuse, but it is not effective for understanding dynamics between intimate partners.

Resource Theory

According to the resource theory explanation of violence between intimate partners, traditional societal norms grant men higher social status and authority over women. Men are in a position of power, have financial resources, access to the public sphere and are supported in their role through culture and social institutions. They hold positions in which they maintain the established order and control the situation. The use of violence is thus posited as the ultimate resource that men may use to keep women, particularly their wives, in line. When men are experiencing a lack of resources, such as income or social status, violence is a means of last resort (Jiwani, 1997). However, it is not obvious why the lack of resources can lead to violence. For example, Lupri, Grandin & Merlin (1994) conducted a survey to examine the relationship between socio-economic status and male violence; their major finding is that there is "... little evidence to suggest that violence in the home is related significantly to income" (p. 68). Men who think they hold a dominant position in their relationship will use violence as the ultimate resource they have to control their wives. From this perspective, women are resources that men can access when they want. The situation is exacerbated when men lose control in their lives at the professional or personal level, thereby jeopardizing their authority. Johnson (1996) states that a large number of men find a contradiction between cultural norms (beliefs regarding men's roles) and the actual situation in which they are living.

Social Control and General Systems Theories

These perspectives view violence as the product of a system, compared to micro-level perspectives that focus on problems of individuals. In a social control perspective, social structures and institutions play an influential role on people's behaviours and affect social conduct (Gelles, 1993). For instance, social prescriptions determine how violence between intimate partners is perceived in our society and sanctioned.

The concept of reciprocity is used to understand the continuation of violence between intimate partners. The reaction to a violent act is seen as crucial in the dynamics between intimate partners, especially for the victim. The responsibility falls on the victim to stop or show a disagreement to a violent incident; if she does not, an abuser will receive positive feedback for committing a violent act and will be encouraged to use violence again (Johnson, 1996).

From this perspective, the lack of sanctions within the justice system towards the first manifestation of violence is key to understanding violence between intimate partners. The criminalization of violence between intimate partners and a harsher punishment of abusers is proposed as a means of reducing violence from the social control perspective. This set of theories argues that men use violence against women when the rewards exceed the costs. This suggests that society in general does not appropriately punish violent behaviour and that men use violence against women because they can. Chamberland (2003) noted that lowered incidence of severe violent acts is correlated with the zero tolerance attitude and criminalization of violence in the United States. However she also pointed out, using Mills' (1996) work, the importance of careful reading and analysis of such a correlation. Criminalization does not necessarily mean efficacy in reducing and eliminating violence between intimate partners. Genuine response to violence has to include as well an intervention to improve conditions for women.

Looking at the issue of sexual assault, Alksnis (2001) illustrates how the legal doctrine, as it has been implemented in the eighties, does not produce an effective response towards the abuser. This researcher suggests that the legal system is not dealing "... with the actual reality of women and children with respect to male sexual violence" (p. 71). Instead, the relationship with the abuser, the severity of the act, and the criminal history of the abuser are the main factors used by the courts to determine the type of crime and degree of sanction. While criminalization is certainly one response to violence between intimate partners and part of a social regulation of behaviour, this solution has to be amalgamated with other types of interventions in order to help the victim, and the abuser as well.

Feminist theory

Feminist theory looks at women's experience, while working towards improving women's social conditions by recognizing inequalities, discrimination, social control and oppression of women. It is through an analysis of the experiences of abusive relationships that feminists are seeking an understanding of violence against women. The main difference between the feminist and the social control perspective is that violence is not considered gender-neutral (Dobash & Dobash, 1998). Violence against women is a product of the patriarchal system, which affords men greater power and prestige than women. In this perspective, it is the historically male-dominated system and institutions that contribute to the subordination of women. Gender and power shape family relationships (Yllo, 1993) and violence is one of the many systemic ways in which women continue to be oppressed within society (Timmins, 1995).

Feminist theory examines institutions (laws, for example) that enable men to use violence against women, as well as the dominant ideologies that support this. The family is seen as a historically situated social institution that was under non-contested male authority. For instance, Guillaumin (1995) has explained women's appropriation in a patriarchal social structure by identifying different mechanisms that allow males to exercise control and power over women. Historically, marriage has been the institution through which women gained social status and identity and became their husband's property. Over the last 30 years, several feminist studies have documented the issue of abusive intimate relationships from the victim's perspective

(Dekeseredy & Macleod, 1997), and have explained the construction of gender and power through social institutions. Feminists have validated women's experience in abusive relationships by developing intervention models that put the emphasis on recognizing personal experience:

> Adopting a feminist analysis will lead the practitioner to denounce violence, to place responsibility for violent acts on the aggressor and to relocate the battered women's problem within the framework of patriarchal society in order to take the blame away from women and relieve immediate tensions (Rinfret-Raynor, et al. 1992, p. 21).

Focusing on women's experiences, feminist researchers and practitioners look at the diversity of women's realities (McGillivray & Comaskey, 1999; Martz & Bryson-Saraurer, 2000). Many feminist works are thus directed at understanding women's experiences and needs (Doherty & Hornosty, 2004; Minaker, 2001).

Connecting the Diversity of Explanations to Intervention Strategies

In this chapter I presented different explanations of violence between intimate partners. This exercise illustrates that understanding the issue through a specific lens will influence the strategies put into place to respond to violence between intimate partners. As mentioned earlier, explaining the causes of violence between intimate partners can be multi-dimensional and may address both individual and social factors. To establish the connection between explanations and intervention strategies, I first asked what focus a theoretical perspective is taking? And second, what period of the lifespan does the particular theory focus on?

For instance, when applying those questions to the micro/individual level explanations, intervention would focus on individuals, treating people on a one-to-one basis in order to change an individual's behaviour. However, this is too simplistic and does not take into account the broader social context addressed outside individual-level approaches. In a psycho-pathological perspective, the emphasis is on the personality traits of the abuser; the problem is located within an individual. Consequently, the strategy correlated with this theory would be to focus on treating a personality disorder, or mental illness. From a social learning perspective the focus is on the behaviour learned by individuals in the family, at school, with friends, from the media, etc. Since violence is learned behaviour, a good way to eradicate it would be to promote prevention in schools, developing programs to improve parents' roles and parenting skills.

In comparison to the psychopathological perspective, social learning explanations suggest implementing an intervention strategy before violence can occur and even before people reach adulthood. The sex role perspective emphasizes the fact that men and women are raised differently and that this socialization has an impact on how they behave and how they perceive the opposite sex. The intervention strategy resulting from this theoretical perspective is to influence sex role learning process with children and to deconstruct sex role stereotypes with adults. From the situational perspective, I have seen that specific events may lead people to use violence against their partner. Loss of control or lack of power over a situation, such as unemployment, death, separation, and illness, are explosive ingredients affecting a person's behaviour. The intervention strategy would thus need to be oriented toward resolving those particular situations, and on ways to deal differently with those than to behave abusively towards a partner. Similarly, if alcohol and drug abuse are seen as direct causes of violence, then we would need to focus interventions on addiction. The problem with micro/individual explanations, in comparison to macro/societal explanations, is that they do not lead to changes in social institutions.

Intervention strategies that emerge from macro/societal-level explanations focus on eradicating systemic violence. Interventions correlated with this perspective focus on the criminalization of violence between intimate partners and facilitating a better community response, on changes in the family institution, safety strategies towards specific groups, or revision of discriminatory policies. Defining the cause of violence by the lifestyle a person adopts, or the environment in which that person evolves, would lead to interventions designed to improve safety in specific environments (e.g., colleges and universities) and groups (e.g., students) that are considered at-risk. The resource perspective also emphasizes strategic interventions with targeted populations (e.g., low income or low education) since violence is seen as caused by a lack of resources. Consequently, interventions may put in place financial programs that would help low-income families to overcome difficult situations, as well as programs to reintegrate people into employment or education systems. As for the social control perspective, it clearly emphasizes changes within the justice and legal system, and the interventions first focus on improving the justice-system response to domestic-violence cases. Training professionals in the justice system is thus a priority from this perspective.

We have seen that acknowledging women's experience and validating their voices is the main focus of the feminist perspective, which has led to the development of an intervention model that specifically empowers women. People sharing this point of view towards violence between intimate partners focus on advocating for better life-conditions for women and on intervening directly with abused women who want to stop the violence. From this perspective, what was once considered to be in the private domain has become public and political. The focus has been on developing services for women, changing laws, and transforming institutions in order to gain equality between men and women.

Looking at the perspectives presented in this chapter has helped make connections with intervention strategies. However, just as it was difficult to delimit the precise boundaries of each perspective, it is hard to establish with certainty which intervention strategy will work best. The fact that there are multiple factors explaining violence between intimate partners calls for a diversity of intervention approaches. What is clear is that gaining a clearer understanding of the various theories is relevant for those who want to design and implement an intervention strategy.

I place the emphasis on *woman abuse* to clearly indicate that violence between intimate partners is not a gender-neutral phenomenon. I find the feminist perspective to be the most promising for framing intervention strategies because of its wide scope, its focus on the validation of women's experiences, and its political character, which holds a greater potential for social change. At the same time, I also recognise that other perspectives can be of value, when intervening in specific aspects related to violence, with particular clients, or at a given point in the lifespan of individuals. In the end, being open to pluralism has more to offer in stopping woman abuse than being rigidly camped in any particular dogmatic position, as long as we have a sound understanding of theories and of their links to intervention strategies.

Notes:

1   The author would like to thank Tina Beaudry-Mellor (Ph.D. candidate at the University of Regina) for her collaboration in preparing the material used in this chapter. Also thanked is Luc Thériault (Associate Professor at the Faculty of Social Work, University of Regina) for his comments on previous versions of this text. Also acknowledged in the preparation of this chapter are Mary R. Hampton and Nikki Gerrard for their editing work on this paper.

2   "L'abus de pouvoir exercé par un où des hommes dans une société où les rapports sociaux de sexe sont inégalitaires et souvent synonymes de domination" (121).

3   Tutty and Goard provide a good discussion about incidence rates on repeated abuse of women by men (2002, p. 14).

4   Under this level of explanation, we combined intra-individual and social psychological theory as delimited by Gelles (1979).

5   Our discussion of theoretical explanations is an overview of specific perspectives and is not inclusive of all approaches.

6   Operant conditioning: "... (step-by-step fashion) is that a victim's compliance with a perpetrator's demands reinforces (rewards) the perpetrator's use of violence" (Barnett, Miller-Perrin & Perrin, 1997, p. 28).

7   Chamberland's view is based on a survey conducted by the Family Violence Laboratory in different years in the United States.

CHAPTER FIVE

Harm Reduction and Abused Women's Safety

Karen M. Nielsen and Ann Marie Dewhurst

Risk and the Abused Woman

The purpose of this chapter is to describe a risk-management framework that we have developed over the past several years. We are a psychologist and clinical social worker who originally came together to discuss our perspectives on family violence. Karen, the social worker, specializes in working with abused women and at the time was supervising a program for men who batter. She has over 20 years of experience in this field. Ann Marie has worked primarily with men who batter and familial-based sexual offenders as well as abused women, also for the past 20 years. The "crime cycle" (Pithers, Marques, Gibat & Marlatt, 1983) and the "behavioural progression framework" used with sexual offenders (Correctional Service of Canada, 2001 — See Table 1) was adapted by her for use in her work with men who batter. We found that it described the dynamics associated with a man's choice to batter and the ways the men managed their abusive behaviour more accurately than the three-stage (Build-up — Explosion — Honeymoon) framework frequently in use with abused women.

As committed feminists working with men who batter, we routinely met with the partners of our clients to inform them about the program.

This reflected our core values that knowledge is empowerment and that the women's safety was paramount. We shared with the women what we knew about abusive men's dynamics. They responded very positively to the behavioural progression model and told us that it fit their own experiences of abuse. It also provided a framework from which they could describe their own experiences. Over time, themes began to emerge from the stories we heard. The first theme was that of *"You described my life."* Comments from women included: "Wow, you really heard me; that's what's been happening to me," "No wonder I'm tired all the time; there's a lot going on here," "I finally get why I feel crazy all the time" and "Leaving will take time but at least I know what's going on."

Table 1: Behavioural Progression of Men Who Batter

Phase	Description
Build-up: (The arousal-building phase)	The abusive man's lifestyle is out of balance and his efforts to gain control are ineffective. He begins to develop a sense of subjective deprivation. As a result, he may feel angry or depressed (Ward, Louden, Hudson & Marshall, 1995). His internal stress levels build and he begins to feel out of control. He manages this need to control by being abusive toward those he considers more vulnerable than himself, i.e., his partner and/or children. He will use control tactics that do not include direct violence. He moves to the next stage when he realizes that his efforts have not had the desired effect.
Acting-out:	This phase is characterized by abusive behaviour and tactics of control (Pense & Paymar, 1986). The abuser experiences some form of gratification for his violence, even though it may be fleeting.
Justification: (of what he has done)	Immediate gratification turns to guilt and shame. To avoid dealing with these feelings, he begins to use cognitive distortions to minimize his responsibility for his actions. He may distort the events by blaming his partner, making her responsible for his actions and her abuse. He may accept partial responsibility by acknowledging that a fight happened but minimizing its seriousness or convincing himself or others that the abuse did not happen at all. Prior to moving to the next stage he makes a resolve that the acting out will never happen again.
Pretend-normal	His account of his abusiveness becomes distorted. If successful in this stage, the abuser may convince himself that "it" will

Table 1: Behavioural Progression of Men Who Batter (cont.)

Phase	Description
Pretend-normal	Not happen again and that everything in his life is "normal." However, because there are no changes to his belief system, lifestyle, or thinking patterns, it is only a matter of time before he re-enters his build-up phase and the cycle continues.

The second major theme was *"I am not alone in this."* Women responded with statements like: "If you can tell me all about this, then it can't just be me" and "You've given me the words to describe this shit." Overall, the women expressed relief that there was something that fit their experience and really helped them understand their partners' decision to be violent.

Of particular help to women was the description of the "pretend-normal phase." We described this as the stage following an abusive episode: when it appears that the incident has ended on the abuser's part but, for the woman, the waiting game begins. She deals with the aftermath of his aggression and waits for things to begin again. Women have often told us that they do feel like they have to "pretend" to be normal after violence. They also described their experiences of this stage as "like walking on eggshells" and "crazy making." This framework allowed for a different dialogue than the discussion of the more commonly described "honeymoon phase." Our clients frequently found that, in their experience, there had never been a "honeymoon phase" or, if there was a time when their abusive partner did try to "make up to them," the attempts ended in the early part of their relationship.

We added components to the original framework over the past eight years. We found it important to add a discussion of how change is made, the risk factors associated with recidivism by men who batter, the goals of change for abused women, and integration of these components into safety planning with women. Eventually, from this evolved our current framework: "Harm Reduction and Abused Women's Safety" (HRAWS).

We have shared this framework with other service providers in both formal and informal settings. We presented it to groups of shelter volunteers and staff and to a provincial symposium on family violence. Additionally, we presented an adapted discussion of HRAWS to a group of service providers from the Gay and Lesbian community. The model was well received in all the venues. The Comprehensive Family Violence Institute implemented the model in 1997. Rita Dillon (personal communication, May 18, 2004), coordinator of the program, provided feedback consistent with our findings. Women in her program found the HRAWS framework a useful teaching tool. It is easily comprehended and appeals to women's common sense. One strength of the framework for these women is that it supports their understanding of the abuser's behaviour without suggesting that the women were responsible for it. We continue to use this framework in our clinical practices.

The HRAWS framework incorporates an understanding of how battered women make changes to reduce risk, as discussed by Brown (1997), with an understanding of the perpetrator's abuse pattern (Kropp, Hart, Webster & Eaves, 1999; Pithers et al., 1983; Ward, Louden, Hudson & Marshall, 1995). The framework offers battered women an opportunity to describe the process they experience in response to their partner's abusive behaviour. A critical analysis of her abuser's abuse progression allows a woman to gain increased control over which coping strategies are most likely to be effective in specific circumstances.

Risk and the Battered Woman: Literature Review

Battering has been defined as the systematic use of violence and abuse to inflict physical, emotional, psychological and sexual harm within an intimate relationship (Pense & Paymar, 1986). The impact of ongoing abuse makes it increasingly difficult for women to make changes, such as leaving an abusive relationship (Browne, 1993: Burstow, 1992). Social factors identified by Jaaber and Dasgupta (http://data.ipharos.com/praxis/documents/AssessingSocialRisk.pdf), such as a woman's experiences with discrimination, poverty, the criminal justice system and the child welfare system, may also detract from her ability to make safety-enhancing changes in her life. Similarly, limitations in a woman's fluency with the dominant language or culture creates barriers to change as isolation increases (for further discussion about this, see Nayyar Javed's chapter in this book). The fear of being marginalized and the reality of limited access to positive social or professional supports also restrict the choices open to an abused woman.

In any event, not all battered women want or are able to end their relationship with an abusive partner. Many women retain hope that their relationships will improve despite ongoing abuse. At least one-third of battered women continue to reside with men who may, and likely will, assault them again (Gondolf, 1998). Additionally, for some women, leaving may also be dangerous. Many women are assaulted or murdered after they leave their abusive partner (Goodman, Koss, Fitzgerald, Russo & Keita, 1993).

He will not change, so what can women do? A common goal for service providers is to support women in the development of an effective safety plan. Cattaneo & Goodman (2003) found that victims of domestic violence are skilled at identifying those partners who will re-abuse. Weisz, Tolman & Saunders (2000) also found that battered women are frequently accurate in predicting if they are likely to be re-abused. Intervention plans need to build on a woman's assessment of her circumstances. Therefore, in order to be helpful, interventions developed with the battered women must focus on expanding the woman's ability to initiate and make changes that enhance her safety.

Simultaneously, the reality that her partner controls her safety must be recognized. Women do not have control over whether their partner will assault them again. Therefore, the goal of change for many women, regardless of whether they leave or stay with an abusive partner, is to reduce the harm they experience (i.e., harm reduction) or to strategically manage, wherever possible, the circumstances that might increase their safety (i.e. risk management). For women living with a man who has a demonstrated history of violence, the goal of harm reduction is to take steps towards reducing risks.

The "risk behaviour" for abused women is having ongoing contact or staying with a partner who has been abusive before and may be again. Harm reduction approaches recognize the difficulty associated with completely eliminating the risk behaviour, yet they encourage incremental steps toward the ideal situation of safety (Kragh & Huber, 2002). However, the harm reduction approach is a pragmatic one that acknowledges that some risks cannot be eliminated in the near future, but at least some of the problems associated with the risk behaviour can be reduced (Des Jarlais, Friedman, Choopanya, Vanichseni & Ward, 1992).

Developing the Harm Reduction — Risk Assessment Framework
The movement toward harm reduction begins with a strong assessment of the risk situation. Harm reduction or risk assessment tools need to gather

information from a variety of sources, and include both static (unchanging or historical) and dynamic (changeable and ongoing) risk factors (Hanson & Bussière, 1998). Women also need tools that help demystify the abuse process and translate this information into meaningful safety planning (McLeod, 1995). We have found that the HRAWS approach supports women in gaining an objective view of their experience, while responsibility for abuse stays with the abuser.

Cattaneo & Goodman (2003) found that women's reports of their risk for being assaulted again was correlated with a number of static (i.e., unchanging or historical) partner variables including: a) a substance abuse problem; b) being generally violent; c) having a tendency toward psychological dominance-isolation. They also included the dynamic variable of the victim's assessment of dangerousness.

Another important factor in supporting a successful change process is to access the right support or intervention at the right time (Prochaska, DiClemente & Norcross, 1992). Brown (1997) proposed the Transtheoretical Model of Change (TMC) as a useful tool for understanding how battered women make changes in their lives. The TMC is composed of five distinct stages: pre-contemplation, contemplation, preparation, action and maintenance (Prochaska, DiClemente & Norcross, 1992; Table 2).

Table 2: The Transtheoretical Model of Change: Stages of Change

Stage	Description
Pre-contemplation	There is no intention to change behaviour in the future. The individual may be unaware or under-aware of their problems.
Contemplation	People are aware that a problem exists and they think about making changes. They have not yet made a commitment to take action. They "know where they want to go but are not quite ready yet." An individual in this stage is in a process of weighing the pros and cons of the problem and the solution to the problem.
Preparation	Individuals in this stage are preparing to take action immediately, or in the near future. They are assessing available information and forming a plan.
Action	Individuals in this stage are putting their plan into action. They are modifying their behaviour or environment in

Table 2: The Transtheoretical Model of Change:
Stages of Change (cont.)

Stage	Description
Action	Order to overcome their problems. The Action stage involves considerable commitment of time and energy.
Maintenance	Strategies are consolidated and improved upon. The primary task is preventing return to past behaviours.

The TMC acknowledges that most people who take action to change their lives do not successfully maintain their gains on the first attempt. Change is made following a spiral process. People can proceed sequentially from one stage to another. However, most people return to an earlier stage or relapse into the problem behaviour (i.e., risk-taking behaviour) before reaching the stage in which changes (i.e., lasting safety in this case) are consolidated and able to be maintained. Each shift to an earlier stage results in some addition to knowledge of self and of the demands of the change process (Prochaska, DiClemente & Norcross, 1992).

The strengths of the TMC are that it enables both service providers and abused women to understand the steps involved in making a change. It also facilitates the identification of barriers likely to be encountered in the change process, and offers suggestions for appropriate interventions at each stage of change. A study investigating the usefulness of the TMC for 12 separate problem areas (e.g., alcoholism, bulimia and smoking cessation) confirmed that it can be applied to people who make significant life, changes either independently or with professional support (Prochaska, Velicer, Rossi, Goldstein, Marcus, et al., 1994). Brown (1997) found that when a battered woman understands how change is made (using the TMC framework), both for herself and her abusive partner, she begins to make more objective decisions about her own life.

Talking about the Problem

Battered women are aware of their partner's progression of abuse and often communicate this information to their service providers when seeking support or shelter. Although they often require encouragement to disclose their experiences of abuse (Riggs, Caulfield & Street, 2000), once they are in a supportive environment, many women can name the stressors, situations and feelings that are associated with their partner's choice to be violent. Additionally, an abused woman can reflect on her coping strategies and determine the effectiveness of her responses to his abuse. Our experience of the disclosures of battered women suggests that abused women experience a pattern of responding to their partner's abusive pattern. This pattern reflects their attempts at coping and resisting abuse. We found that women observe their partner's behaviour and respond in ways they believe will de-escalate his build-up process. Table 3 describes the process; we have developed this model that integrates theoretical knowledge and practical experience.

Table 3: The Process Experienced by Battered Women Paralleling the Abuser's Progression

Abuse cycle stage	Battered woman	Abusive man
Build-up	Awareness of partner's tension-building process increases. Vigilance and ongoing monitoring increases. More attention paid to detail. Tries to contain partner's negative affect. Personal tension builds. Becomes more reactive to the coping style of partner. Notices her attempts to cope are not working as well as before. Personal needs are forgone in favour of meeting partner's needs (e.g., she gives up financial independence, family, friends, mobility, spirituality, etc.). May attempt to gain some control using some of partner's abusive tactics. Begins to take on responsibility for partner's behaviour. Manages feelings resulting from taking responsibility for her partner's feelings and actions. Shifts her reality to match her circumstances.	Event triggers tension-building process. Personal coping mechanisms insufficient to manage feelings. Attempts to cope include the use of control tactics, substance abuse and other forms of acting out. Tendency to rely on his support system to do emotional work for him. Broods about difficulties, looks externally for their causes and for relief. Escalates blaming and reduces personal responsibility. Reverts to stereotypic social responses. Seeks validation in male privilege. Deliberately escalates use of control tactics against partner, including isolation, economic, spiritual, physical, sexual, emotional and intellectual abuse.

Table 3: The Process Experienced by Battered Women Paralleling the Abuser's Progression (cont.)

Abuse cycle stage	Battered woman	Abusive man
Act-out	Survives the use of intimidation, threats of violence, indirect violence, sexual abuse and direct violence. Shifts her reality to match her circumstances.	Uses intimidation, threats of violence, indirect violence, sexual abuse and/or physical violence directed at partner. Minimizes, denies and blames others for his abusive actions and emotional state.
Justification	Manages the emotional and physical aftermath of abuse. Interprets abuser's behaviour to make sense of the experience. Resolves to "try harder or leave next time." Seeks out messages or support to stay, confront or leave depending upon her resources and opportunity. Shifts her reality to match her circumstances.	Manages the shame and guilt he experiences following episodes of abuse. Returns to defence mechanisms. Promises to "never do it again" and decides that the abuse is "in the past" and to be happy he must "put the events behind him."
Pretend-normal	Continues to care for partner and home, to defend and protect others. Pretends everything is okay. Becomes "crazy," ill, "hysterical," drunk, dead, etc. Shifts her reality to match her circumstances.	Pretends that his relationship is a normal one and that everything is okay.

By itself, an analysis of the abuser's abusive pattern and the battered woman's coping pattern is not enough to help her. Although many women are able accurately to assess the danger, they may express a belief that reflects too much confidence in their ability to get away from their abuser. For example, Martin et al. (2000) found that battered women often believe they are less likely than the "average battered woman" to return to the abusive relationship. Alternatively, women faced with the reality of their situation may become hopeless about their ability to make change and do not take potential steps toward safety (McLeod, 1995). An effective harm reduction or risk management tool must also reflect a woman's readiness for change and offer options for safe interventions.

The Framework: Harm Reduction and Abused Women's Safety (HRAWS)

What Is It?

The purpose of this harm reduction-risk management framework is to facilitate a change process. It is not intended to be a lethality assessment or a tool to predict a recurrence of abuse. As a descriptive tool, the data gathered through this framework can: a) validate the woman's experience of the danger existing in her relationship; b) identify the level of urgency with which specific changes need to be addressed; and, c) identify the stage of change that best describes the woman in the here and now.

How Do We Use the Tool?

We propose a harm reduction-risk management framework that service providers can use with women. Following the HRAWS framework, service providers use the following steps when counselling or supporting victims of battering: a) review with the woman her experiences of abuse and her awareness of her partner's abuse progression; b) using her knowledge of her partner's behavioural progression, explore what types of interventions the woman can make to increase her safety; c) review with the woman her previous change attempts and her beliefs about what changes need to be made in her life; d) help the woman identify her stage of change; e) explore interventions which facilitate her move toward the next stage of change; and f) periodically re-evaluate the change process to ensure that the path the woman is on will meet her goals and maintain her safety.

As a first step, we describe the behavioural progression of violence to the woman. We do this in a story-telling manner, reflecting to her that we have learned this story from listening to the experiences of many abused women. It is important to use a flip chart and draw the story (i.e., drawing and labelling the four parts of the pattern and defining the components of each phase) while describing the progression (Figure 1).

The woman is then invited to describe her experiences. The helper can support her in linking her story to the progression framework. A helper can

Figure 1. The abuse progression diagram

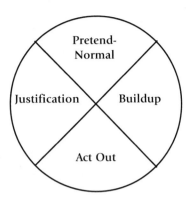

listen for examples of the woman's resilient responses to the abuse. Bowker (1993) describes many of the ways that women demonstrate their resiliency through resisting abuse. The helper also listens for the meaning a woman has given to her experiences of violence, e.g., "this is a punishment for not being a good person" or "I am a good person but my husband has an alcohol problem." This is an opportunity to clarify beliefs and use re-framing to link her meaning back to the resiliencies identified. The helper should also listen for descriptions of the social barriers the woman has experienced, and ask her about the impact of the physical, psychological, emotional and spiritual trauma. Through this dialogue, the counselling or support option recommendations can be developed, as well as a safety plan that minimizes risk. This information will also provide important feedback regarding the woman's stage of change

How Will it Help Women?
As a strategic tool, the data gathered through this framework can: a) validate the woman's "here-and-now" experience in the context of her whole life; b) support the woman in identifying and expanding her capacity for changing her world; c) identify the woman's coping strategies and strengths; d) support the woman in building and maintaining hope; and e) identify both short- and long-term goals and strategies with the woman.

As women gain information that validates their observations and reactions, they can be more effective in predicting episodes of violence and more strategic in their actions. For example, abuse of alcohol is a common correlate with the onset of violence. If a woman understands that her partner's "trip to the bar with the guys" is part of his build-up phase and an indicator that she is still in a pre-contemplation stage of change, she can decide to seek shelter while he is at the bar. Prior to engaging in the risk management assessment, she may have waited until he came home, hoping that "this time" it would be different.

Planning with the new risk management model can be done whether the battered woman chooses to remain within her relationship or engage in the leaving process. Supporting a woman in the evaluation of elements that comprise her risk, and the management of her risk, allows for a dialogue of change to continue. An example of such a change is the woman shifting her belief that abuse is somehow connected to her behaviour to an understanding that her partner is solely responsible for his choice to be violent. This demonstrates a move from pre-contemplation into contemplation and perhaps the readiness to move into a preparation stage of change.

Timing Is Everything

Good service or important information offered at the wrong time may not be recognized as helpful, and may increase the woman's feeling of powerlessness or hopelessness. For example, pressuring the woman described previously to leave her partner, when she has only recently challenged his blaming her for his abuse, ignores her need to contemplate and prepare. It pushes her too quickly into a dramatic action that may be too big a change and feel too intimidating. She may then start to avoid the support system, as she feels guilty for not changing. What the support system has inadvertently done is increase her risk by facilitating the woman's isolation.

Well-timed services can facilitate movement from one stage to the next (see Table 2). For example, the major task in moving from the preparation stage into the action stage is consciousness-raising. This involves battered women defining and becoming educated about abuse in general and their partner's behavioural progression in particular. The focus becomes moving from stage to stage rather than leaving the relationship. Movement from stage to stage is entirely within the woman's control, unlike her partner's abusive behaviour.

Conclusion

Understanding the abuse progression and the change process can help a battered woman to expand her options. As demonstrated by the Transtheoretical Model of Change, the more information and options available, the more likely a person is to move through preparation into action with a well-constructed plan (Prochaska, et al. 1994). A combination of the Transtheoretical Model of Change and the adapted cycle of abuse (Dewhurst & Nielsen, 1997) is a powerful construct that can enhance the woman's ability to make changes as safely as possible. Understanding of the batterer's abuse progression, and the many ways that a woman is affected by it, increases a woman's ability to make effective changes in her life. It also enhances her ability to identify and manage risks to her safety. Knowledge about the batterer's behavioural progression will not prevent future violence, but it does mean that a woman can be more efficient in her defence strategies. Increased understanding deepens a woman's awareness and thus informs her action. She is empowered to set her own pace for change. When the same understanding is shared with people in her support system, they are more able to provide appropriate support that matches the woman's pace. They can then provide more effective help.

CHAPTER SIX

"Over Policed and Under Protected": *A Question of Justice for Aboriginal Women*

Jane Ursel

> The issue of family violence is the most complex terrain upon which to determine what constitutes justice. Historically, we are at the juncture of powerful countervailing forces ... victims and women's groups are commending the criminalization of family violence and Aboriginal organizations and advocates are championing the cause of alternative justice and decriminalization. Aboriginal women and their advocates often find themselves caught between these countervailing views. While both sides agree that abuse must end ... they clearly do not agree on the means by which this might be achieved. (Submission to the Aboriginal Justice Inquiry Implementation Commission, 2001)

In October of 2004, Amnesty International released a report entitled, *Stolen Sisters: A Human Rights Response to Discrimination and Violence Against Indigenous Women in Canada*. The report focused primarily on cities in Western Canada where there is a large and growing Indigenous population and where there have been a number of highly publicized incidents of violence against Indigenous women.

Most Canadians are familiar with Amnesty International's work in Third World and war-torn countries and support its efforts to end violence, discrimination, and human rights abuses in those distant, less privileged nations. To have the same critical lens turned upon us, and to find our country singled out for international censure, is an unfamiliar and disturbing experience. The report states that "Canadian authorities have failed in their responsibility to protect the rights of Indigenous women in Canada" and they cite the following factors which led to this condemnation:

- Despite assurances to the contrary, police in Canada have often failed to provide Indigenous women with an adequate standard of protection.
- The resulting vulnerability of Indigenous women has been exploited by Indigenous and non-Indigenous men to carry out acts of extreme brutality against them.
- These acts of violence may be motivated by racism, or may be carried out in the expectation that societal indifference to the welfare and safety of Indigenous women will allow the perpetrators to escape justice. (*Stolen Sisters*, 2004, p. 1)

I suggest that this report is so unsettling not only because it reveals an ugly reality in Canadian society but also because the information the report reveals has become part of the debate in our country; this information is deeply divisive and has touched a very raw nerve. The question of how best to respond to violence against women, especially Aboriginal women, is extremely controversial when applied to the issue of family violence. Among a people who have justifiably felt "over policed and under protected," the role of the criminal justice system in domestic violence situations is heavily laden with a history of colonization, oppression and the destruction of Aboriginal families and communities.

The Fault Line

In the early 1980s, advocates for abused women were critical of the historic indifference of the justice system to crimes of violence within the family. They challenged the "double standard" within a society in which hitting a stranger was a crime, while hitting a family member was a "personal" problem. They called for an end to this double standard and demanded that people who assault family members be treated as seriously by the police and the courts as people who assault strangers. "Criminal processing of people who assault family members reaffirms social disapproval of violence, and it also, at least in theory, subjects violent people to interventions that might deter, incapacitate or rehabilitate them" (Worden, 2000, p. 217).

While victims' and women's movements were advocating criminalization of domestic-violence offenders, there was an equally committed movement calling for decriminalization of actions and individuals deemed over-represented in the criminal justice system (CJS). Some of the strongest voices for decriminalization were advocates for alternative justice for Aboriginal people. These advocates, including the authors of the *Aboriginal Justice Inquiry Report*, identified the massive over-representation of Aboriginal people in the criminal justice system and argued that arrests and imprisonment were foreign to Aboriginal concepts of justice and redress and therefore were not effective in rehabilitation (Hamilton & Sinclair, 1991; Nuffield, 1998; LaPrairie, 1996; York, 1992). The debate over criminal justice interventions in cases of family violence among Aboriginal people occurs at all levels of our society, from grass-roots women's organizations, to band councils, to the Canadian Parliament, to the Supreme Court of Canada.

In 1996, amendments to the Canadian Criminal Code were made in response to concerns about the over-representation of Aboriginal people in our prisons; section 718.2(e) on sentencing principles stated that "all available sanctions other than imprisonment that are reasonable in the circumstances should be considered for all offenders, with particular attention to the circumstances of Aboriginal offenders." In 1999, the Supreme Court of Canada released a judgment on section 718.2(e) in the case of *R. v. Gladue*. This is of particular interest because it involved a domestic homicide. The Supreme Court ruling indicated that section 718.2(e) required a new framework of analysis that sentencing judges must consider, with two focus points:

- The unique systemic or background factors which may have played a part in bringing the particular Aboriginal offender before the courts; and
- The types of sentencing procedures and sanctions which may be appropriate in circumstances for the offender because of his or

her particular Aboriginal heritage or connection. (April 23,1999) Doc.26300,23 C.R. (5th)197,133 C.C.C. (3d) 385 (S.C.C.).

In a case comment, Campbell states that "... the Court notes that there is no intention to create a separate justice system for Aboriginal people. The court notes that the more serious or violent the crime, the less likely it may be that the sentence will differ as between an Aboriginal and a non-Aboriginal offender" (Campbell 1999, p. 240).

The criminal code amendment on sentencing (1996) and the Supreme Court decision *R. v. Gladue* (1999) affirm the special consideration owed to Aboriginal people by virtue of their historic disenfranchisement. However, it is notable that in cases of serious and violent crimes the Supreme Court anticipates that the special considerations of Aboriginal background may be outweighed by the need for protection and security. This is the "fault line" that frequently divides the Aboriginal community by gender. Aboriginal women victims and their advocates express strong concern about tendencies to decriminalize domestic assaults for Aboriginal people (McGillivray, 1997; McIvor and Nahanee, 1998; LaRocque, 1995). LaRocque articulates the concern that failure to intervene in crimes of Aboriginal people against Aboriginal people abandons victims, who are set up to live lives of silent pain, fear and continual victimization.

> Those involved in gross and willful crimes should receive very lengthy jail sentences and in specific cases, should also be permanently removed from their communities. In cases of brutalization, rape and ruthless murder, removal may be the only effective measure of protection for victims and their families, especially in small and/or remote settlements (LaRocque, 1995, p. 116–117).

Canadian studies have consistently reported high rates of victimization among Aboriginal women and children (Ontario Native Women's Association, 1989; Canadian Panel of Violence Against Women, 1993; Comack, 1993; Proulx & Perrault, 2000). Statistics Canada reports that Aboriginal women are victimized at three times the rate of non-Aboriginal women and twice the rate of Aboriginal men (Statistics Canada, 1999). Many of these studies link the specific prevalence and nature of family violence in Aboriginal communities to their experience of colonization, the legacy of residential schools and the consequent pattern of intergenerational abuse. In short, from an historic stand point it is difficult to separate the victims and the abusers because of the profound history of abuse of Aboriginal people. From the standpoint of Aboriginal offenders (who may have been abused as children) the question arises: do they merit a different consequence because of their history? From the standpoint of Aboriginal women, the weight of history and the urgency of immediate risk seem to pull in different directions. Do Aboriginal victims merit greater police intervention because of their greater risk (as Amnesty International implies), or less police intervention because of their assailants history of abuse[1]? Much of the debate seems to revolve around the question of whether we privilege past or present victims.

How do we respond to the critiques of Amnesty International and provide greater protection to Aboriginal women without fuelling the over-criminalization of Aboriginal people? It is important to note that many of the criticisms made in *Stolen Sisters* were levelled at policing in Canada. Because most assaults against women and most female homicides are perpetrated by intimate partners (Statistics Canada, 2004), this chapter will focus on domestic violence policies, particularly the Winnipeg Police Service's "zero tolerance policy" and its impact on Aboriginal women. It is a very controversial policy which prioritizes safety and minimizes police discretion. We will explore what lessons can be learned from this policy and whether it provides an answer, in part, to Amnesty International's demand that greater protection be provided to Aboriginal women.

To explore these questions we will use data from the Winnipeg Family Violence Court[2] (FVC) that were collected over a period of eight years from 1992 to 2000. The data were collected from all incoming domestic violence matters in which an arrest was made. We are dealing with a complete population of family violence cases rather than a sample. The only missing cases are those in which the accused died or is out on warrant and the case is not meaning.

Status of Manitoba Justice Policy on Domestic Violence

Over the past two decades a series of policy and legislative changes have been designed to increase justice interventions in family violence matters.

The following reforms are of particular interest in the evolution of Winnipeg's policing policy:

- 1983 — The Attorney General of Manitoba issued a directive to charge, to the police forces in Manitoba, stating that when there are reasonable and probable grounds to indicate that a crime has occurred the police must charge regardless of the relationship between the victim and the accused.
- 1990 — Development of the specialized criminal court for family violence cases, referred to as the Family Violence Court (FVC), which provides specialized prosecutors and designated courts for family violence matters, was developed.
- 1992 — A specialized correctional program, which provides trained counsellors or correctional officers to run batterers treatment groups for court-mandated offenders was instituted.
- 1993 — The "zero tolerance policy" was adopted by the Winnipeg Police Service.
- 1999 — The Domestic Violence and Stalking Protection, Prevention and Compensation Act was created.
- 2000 — Manitoba Corrections introduced a special unit at Headingley prison for domestic violence offenders.

In the context of these dramatic changes in the CJS response to domestic violence cases, a lively debate has emerged on the merits of pro-arrest policies throughout North America. While academics have become increasingly divided on the issue of arrest, it is important to note that service providers working in the field of domestic violence and the general public (when surveyed) continue to support pro-arrest policies (Johnson & Sigler, 1995; Ursel & Brickey, 1996). In Winnipeg, random sample surveys were conducted in 1984 (after the 1983 directive), in 1991 (after the development of FVC), and in 1995 (after zero tolerance), to assess public attitudes to these policy changes. These surveys indicated very high levels of support for Criminal Justice System interventions in family violence cases.

Table 1: Public Attitudes to Policy Changes in the Criminal Justice System Winnipeg Area Study 1984, 1991, and 1995

	Total sample agree	Women agree	Men agree
1983 Directive to Charge	85%	87%	85%
Family Violence Court	89%	91%	87%
Zero Tolerance Policy	80%	87%	71%

Arrest Practices

Throughout the period of policy change, from the directive to charge in 1983 to the introduction of zero tolerance in 1993, arrest rates for spousal assaults have risen dramatically. A third factor that had an impact on arrest rates was the introduction of the Family Violence Court. These 3 factors combined to increase the arrests for spouse abuse from 629 in 1983 to a peak of 3,842 in 1999-2000. When we examine the characteristics of the persons arrested, we find that the majority of the offenders are men (85 percent) and the majority of the victims are women (85 percent). Of the 22,737 individuals arrested for spouse[3] abuse in the eight-year period 1992 to 2000, 8,660 or 38 percent were Aboriginal and 14,077 or 62 percent were non-Aboriginal. Current population estimates indicate that people of Aboriginal origin constitute approximately 12 to 13 percent of Winnipeg's population while they make up 38 percent of the arrests for domestic violence. Aboriginal people are over-represented by a factor of three in the family violence court, which is consistent with the Statistics Canada victimization survey that indicated Aboriginal women were three times more likely to suffer from spousal assault than non-Aboriginal women, and twice as likely to be victimized from all forms of assault than Aboriginal men (Statistics Canada, 1999 General Social Survey on Victimization). Table 2 gives a brief comparative description of case characteristics by ethnicity.

Table 2 indicates that in many regards the characteristics of Aboriginal and non-Aboriginal cases are similar. The overwhelming majority of accused are men and the overwhelming majority of the victims are women. The age at arrest is also very similar. The one outstanding difference is the socio-economic status of the two groups. The majority of Aboriginal accused (66 percent) were on social assistance and the majority of the non-Aboriginal

Table 2: Characteristics of Spouse Abuse Cases Resulting in Arrest by Ethnicity of Accused — Winnipeg 1992-2000

	Aboriginal		Non-Aboriginal	
	Number	Percentage	Number	Percentage
Sex of Accused				
Male	7,073	82%	11,931	85%
Female	1,577	18%	2,131	15%
Male and Female	10	<1%	15	<1%
Sex of Victim				
Male	1,508	17%	2,089	15%
Female	6,981	81%	11,662	83%
Male & Female	171	2%	326	2%
Employment Status				
Employed	1,883	25%	7,216	57%
Unemployed	1,006	13%	1,679	13%
Social Assistance	4,479	59%	3,130	25%
Other*	254	3%	614	5%
Median Age of Accused	30 years		32 years	

*The other category includes student, homemaker and retired.

accused (53 percent) were employed. These statistics reflect the tremendously disadvantaged economic status of Aboriginal people in Canada today. It also reflects the reality, observed in most criminal justice studies, that the majority of people who come to the attention of the law are people of low socio-economic status. This is true of the non-Aboriginal accused as well, who exhibit a much lower employment rate and a much higher rate of dependence on social assistance than the adult male population of Winnipeg. This raises the concern about class/ethnic bias in the criminal justice system and the extent to which zero tolerance reflects or contributes to this bias.

Class/Ethnic Bias and Policing

A school of thought that is critical of criminal justice intervention and particularly pro-arrest policies is articulated by a Canadian sociologist, Noreen Snider, who is concerned about the over-criminalization of low-income people. "Lower income, visible minority, and Aboriginal women have paid a heavy price for mandatory criminalization. It is primarily their communities ... that are targeted for enhanced surveillance" (Snider 1998, p. 146). A Canadian historian, Carol Strange (1995, p. 301), states: "Historical evidence of battered wives' strategies confirms that women avoid the criminal courts whenever alternatives are available."

Yet every year in Winnipeg, a city of 670,000 people, thousands of women call the police requesting protection from abusive spouses. A further 500 to 800 seek protection by applying for a protection order through the new Domestic Violence and Stalking Prevention, Protection and Compensation Act. Even with the recent option of a specific civil remedy, the calls to the Winnipeg police have increased over time. The Winnipeg police recorded over 14,000 calls of a domestic nature in 2000.

The Winnipeg police data reveal a number of important matters. Despite the fact that calling the police is usually a woman's last choice, more and more women in Winnipeg are calling the police. Further, the majority of these calls (60 percent of all calls) are in two districts that have a high ratio of low income individuals and a high ratio of Aboriginal households. We know from the FVC data that the majority of these calls are made by the victim herself.

Given that, in most cases, the police are not women's first choice for help, why are so many women, particularly Aboriginal women, calling the police. Two factors appear to explain this: first, the lack of alternatives; and second, the imminence of danger. *The Canadian Violence Against Women Survey* found that "(a) battered woman's decision to involve police is related to the severity of the violence and whether children are involved ... A woman is three times as likely to call the police if she had children who witnessed the violence, four times as likely if she was injured, and five times as likely if she fears her life is in danger" (Johnson 1996, p. 142–144).

McGillivray and Comaskey (1996) report similar findings in their interviews with Aboriginal women in Winnipeg: "The most frequent reason for calling police was fear for her safety and that of her children ... 'I was really afraid that he would get really out of hand, worse than the last time.' 'The reasons I contacted the police was because he was abusing me, he was hitting me, accusing me. And he was scaring the girls.' 'I wanted him to pay for hurting me.' 'I wanted him out of my home.'" (p. 95).

Table 3: Person Who Called the Police in Domestic Assault Cases by Ethnicity of the Accused — Winnipeg 1992–2000

	All cases		Aboriginal		Non-Aboriginal	
	Number	%	Number	%	Number	%
Victim	16,682	79%	6,155	77%	10,527	80%
Accused*	1,267	6%	403	5%	864	7%
Child	435	2%	193	2%	242	2%
Other Family	499	2%	236	3%	263	2%
Third Party	2,246	11%	1,010	13%	1,236	9%

*Cases in which the accused call the police typically involve cases of dual arrests.

The debate and controversy over appropriate police intervention in low income communities is a long-standing debate. From the standpoint of low income or Aboriginal accused there is the expressed concern that they are more likely to "suffer" police intervention for behaviour that would not result in police intervention in a middle-class community (Snider, 1998). This concern is supported by data from our criminal courts, including the Winnipeg FVC, which consistently show that low income and Aboriginal people are over-represented in the criminal justice system. However, from the standpoint of low income or Aboriginal victims there is the expressed concern that they are more likely to "suffer" victimization and typically their only source of help is the police (McGillivray & Comaskey, 1996; LaRocque, 1993). Thus, the over-representation of low income or Aboriginal people in our FVC is a reflection of the limited resources available to actual or potential victims. Given that police are often their only resource for protection, to limit or remove that support would result in putting many more women's lives at risk, particularly low income or Aboriginal women.

In assessing how great that risk would be, information on the nature of the crime and the prior record rate of the accused is helpful in gauging how potentially dangerous an accused could be. Table 4 provides information on two important risk indicators by ethnicity of the accused: 1) whether they used or threatened use of a weapon; and 2) whether they had a prior record for violence.

Table 4: Weapon Use and Prior Record Rate for Spouse Abuse Cases by Ethnicity of Accused Winnipeg Family Violence Court; September 1992 to September 2000

Ethnicity	Weapon use*		Prior record		Prior record for crimes against persons		Prior record for domestic abuse	
	N	%	N	%	N	%	N	%
Aboriginal	1,772	21%	7,500	92%	6,119	75%	3,832	47%
non-Aboriginal	2,391	17%	9,768	75%	6,807	52%	4,087	31%

*A single code is used in our data collection for threat and use of a weapon. A weapon must be visible during the assault for it to be included in the weapon code.

Given that weapon use and prior history of violence are key risk indicators, the above table suggests that a significant percentage of the persons arrested had a high potential to be dangerous, and that Aboriginal accused were significantly higher in the risk indicators than non-Aboriginal accused. These findings suggest that Winnipeg women had substantial reason to fear for their safety and their call to the police was a call for protection.

The only way to reduce the over-representation of Aboriginal people at the entry level of the justice system is to respond to Aboriginal women's calls for help differently than to those from non-Aboriginal women. Studies cited earlier indicate that Aboriginal women do not want to be treated differently than non-Aboriginal women, particularly when they are at risk. To try to reduce the over-representation of Aboriginal people in FVC by reducing the number of arrests, would have the effect of reducing protection to Aboriginal women and children. In short, we would be ignoring current victims in an attempt to counteract historic injustices. While it is important to address these historic injustices to Aboriginal peoples, to do so at the policing level in domestic violence cases would have the effect of creating or perpetuating a whole new generation of victims.

Discretion

The zero tolerance policy in Winnipeg grew out of a judicial inquiry into a domestic matter which ended in murder. *The Pedlar Report* (1991) observed that police response to domestic calls was inconsistent and recommended that Manitoba police forces introduce policies that would clarify the police's role and responsibilities when called to a domestic incident. Pedlar's observations are substantiated by numerous studies that indicate that police effectively drew a boundary around what they considered legitimate work ("real crime"), and dealt with all other incidents at their own discretion (Black & Reiss, 1967). Researchers reported uneven compliance with early attempts to increase arrests for domestic cases (Ferraro, 1989; Lawrenz, Lembo & Schade, 1988; Mignon & Holmes, 1995).

Research on "Aboriginal Victims of Crime," for the Aboriginal Justice Inquiry, highlights the danger of relying on police discretion to charge: "... concern was raised that police officers do not respond to crimes seriously when they involve native women who are intoxicated because it is felt they are responsible for their own victimization" (Van der Put, 1990 p. 18). There is a very real concern among victims and their advocates that police discretion means privileging white, middle-class women who conform to an idea of the "deserving" victim. Studies and reports of past police practice give evidence that such concerns are well-founded.

Numerous studies have documented diversity in officers' attitudes about domestic violence (e.g., Homant & Kennedy, 1985; Dolon, Hendricks & Meagher 1986; Friday, Metzgar & Walters, 1991; Belknap, 1995). Further, these studies indicate that police attitudes influence police response and action (Bonnycastle & Rigakos, 1998; Dobash & Dobash, 1998; Ericson, 1982). McGillivray and Comaskey (1996) document the particular concern Aboriginal women have about police attitudes. Aboriginal women interviewed by Comaskey and McGillivray reported experiences of police not believing them, police judging them, police blaming them for their own victimization: "I've always called the police. As a matter of fact, one time when I called the police, the staff sergeant was upset with me. He says, 'I'm getting pretty upset with you, you're always phoning, calling here, you're getting to be a bloody nuisance . . . I should charge you for harassing, phoning here all the time" (p. 96).

Pro-arrest policies are designed to take attitudes out of action and clarify the role of the police (Buel, 1988). However, one Canadian study actually revealed an improvement of police officers' attitudes towards victims as a result of pro-arrest policies. Jaffe's et al. (1991) study of a rigorous arrest policy in London, Ontario found favourable attitude changes among police officers, increased reporting rates, and subsequent satisfaction with both the police and the courts by battered women (Jaffe et al., 1991). While the development of a sympathetic attitude towards the victim is ideal, currently the most important aspect of zero tolerance is the mandate to respond rapidly and to arrest, in circumstances of reasonable and probable cause that a crime occurred.

Some critics of pro-arrest policies have argued that they cause more harm than good because they have increased the incidence of dual arrests or double charging (Comack, Chopyk & Wood, 2000; Martin, 1997). A dual arrest typically occurs when police respond to a domestic call and both the husband and the wife allege that the other person assaulted them. However, the magnitude of that increase may not be significant enough to undermine the effectiveness of the policy. In 1992–93, prior to the zero tolerance policy, arrest data indicated that in 94 percent of the domestic violence calls which police attended and a charge was laid, only one person was charged, and three years after the policy 92 percent of cases resulted in a single person being charged. As Table 5 below indicates the year prior to zero tolerance, 6 percent of domestic arrests involved dual charges and the years subsequent to zero tolerance, 7 to 8 percent of domestic arrests involved dual charges. An increase of 1 to 2 percent does not suggest that zero tolerance caused dual arrests. However, this should not lead to the conclusion that dual arrests are not a matter of concern.

Although dual arrests occur in 7 to 8 percent of households, this results in 14 to 15 percent of the cases before the courts because 2 persons are charged. The consequences of dual arrests are very troubling. If a woman's call for help results in her arrest, police punish rather than protect her. This is clearly not the intent of the zero tolerance policy. This could seriously discourage the particular woman from calling the police again when she is at risk and could operate as a deterrent to many women who become aware of the possibility of a dual arrest.

Table 5: Incidence of Dual Arrests In Spouse Abuse Cases*
Winnipeg Family Violence Court 1992–2000

Year	Number of spouse abuse analyzed	Couples		Individuals	
	Number	Number	%	Number	%
1992–93	2,959	168	6%	335	11%
1993–94	3,319	239	7%	478	14%
1994–95	2,888	190	7%	388	13%
1995–96	2,854	229	8%	457	16%
1996–97	2,670	211	8%	421	16%
1997–98	2,631	243	9%	486	18%
1998–99	2,616	233	9%	466	18%
1999–00	3,221	292	9%	584	18%
Total	23,158	1,805	8%	3,615	16%

* Note: The numbers in this table are larger than our data set for spouse abuse because we included "other" family assaults. These cases also have incidents of dual arrest which are of concern.

Given the concern that Aboriginal women have identified, about being believed by the police, it is important to determine whether Aboriginal families are over-represented in the dual arrest category. A review of our data by ethnicity of the accused and/or complainant indicates that Aboriginal families are not at greater risk of dual arrest. Overall, 38 percent of the FVC cases involve persons of Aboriginal origin; however, 33 percent of the dual arrest cases involve these families. Thus Aboriginal families are slightly less likely to be subject to dual arrest than all other families.

Does Zero Tolerance Provide Protection?

To return to the Amnesty International Report, they cite a 2003 UN report on violence against women which calls upon governments to "... prevent, investigate and punish acts of all forms of violence against women, whether in the home, the workplace, the community or society...." The FVC data does demonstrate that police are responding more rapidly to domestic calls for help and they are increasing their arrests of accused offenders. Further, data indicate that more women, particularly more Aboriginal women, are calling the police and as a result more Aboriginal men are being arrested. The critical test is: are women being protected by this policy? This is a more difficult test but there are some preliminary indications that the zero tolerance policy is protecting women. It is generally recognized by service providers and researchers that it is unreasonable to expect that a single intervention, in a single case, at a single point in time will "solve" a complex problem like family violence. However, there is an underlying assumption that greater accessibility to support/intervention programs will, over time, reduce victims' vulnerability. If we use this modest "incrementalist" criteria to measure success in policing, two sources of national data provide indicators of reduced violence towards women.

In the first case, we see evidence from national victimization surveys that between the 1993 and 1999 surveys there was a 28 percent increase of women reporting to police when they were assaulted, and overall a 33 percent reduction in women who self-reported having been abused (Statistics Canada, 2000, p. 19–20). These results hold up the hope that early police interventions may reduce escalation and prevent more serious assaults.

The second source of data is Canadian homicide statistics, which indicate a reduction in spousal homicides during the period of the expanding pro-arrest policies in Canada. National rates of spousal homicide for both women and men have decreased by about half since data collection began in 1974. The homicide rate for women dropped from 16.5 per million married women in 1974 to 8.1 in 2002 and the rate for men decreased from 4.4 to 2.0 (Statistics Canada, 2004, p. 36). Regional breakdowns of these data from 1993 to 2002 (a period which coincides with the zero tolerance policy in Winnipeg) indicate that, in general, spousal homicides are higher in western Canada with the exception of Manitoba, which had the third lowest homicide rate for women in all of Canada. While the ten-year national average was 7.9 per million female victims, the Manitoba rate was 6.9 per million female victims. It is interesting to note that in the region that reported the lowest rate of women calling police and the lowest police arrest rate, the Yukon (Statistics Canada, 2000), the ten-year homicide rate for women was 37.5 per million (Statistics Canada, 2004). While these statistics are not as precise as we would like (they do not provide ethnic breakdowns), they do provide some validation to the assumption that more responsive policing will provide greater protection to women. This is a significant correlation, given Amnesty International's observation: "According to a 1996 Canadian government statistic, Indigenous women between the ages of 25 and 44 with status under the federal Indian Act, are five times more likely than other women of the same age to die as the result of violence." (Amnesty International, 2004, p. 9).

Thus, at this stage, statistics seem to indicate that the zero tolerance policy is more effectively responding to Aboriginal women's calls for assistance than previous police practices. The remaining and most difficult question is: Can we respond to the call for greater police protection without fueling the criminalization of Aboriginal people?

The Consequences of a High Arrest Rate

As a result of high arrest rates, more family violence offenders and particularly more Aboriginal offenders are coming to the attention of the courts. Recalling the amendments to the Canadian Criminal Code on sentencing principles, drawing attention to the special circumstances of Aboriginal offenders and the Supreme Court decision in the case of *R. v. Gladue* discussed previously, we are reminded of the dilemma we face in Canada. Our judges are being advised by the Criminal Code of Canada and the Supreme Court to "use all available sanctions other than imprisonment that are reasonable, with particular attention to the circumstances of Aboriginal offenders." However, they are also advised that "the more serious or violent the crime, the less likely it may be that the sentence will differ between an Aboriginal and a non-Aboriginal offender." This contradiction is perfectly encapsulated in cases of domestic violence, where the risks are high and the probability of escalation is significant.

Despite the above rulings and advice, we find that sentences do differ for Aboriginal and non-Aboriginal offenders in Family Violence Court. While Aboriginal and non-Aboriginal accused are convicted at approximately the same rate, the sentences for Aboriginal offenders are significantly different. The most frequent sentence for spouse abuse in FVC is supervised probation. Overall, we find little difference by ethnicity in sentences to supervised probation; 61 percent of Aboriginal offenders and 62 percent of non-Aboriginal offenders are sentenced to supervised probation. The two outcomes in which ethnicity appears to be a factor are the most and least serious sentences, i.e. incarceration and conditional discharge. Table 6 identifies all sentence outcomes by ethnicity of the offender.

Table 6: Sentences of Spouse Abuse Offenders by Ethnicity*
Winnipeg 1992–2000

	Aboriginal		Non-Aboriginal	
	Number	Percentage	Number	Percentage
Cases Proceeding to Sentence	4,475		6,265	
Incarceration	1,416	32%	1,141	18%
Conditional Sentence	21	<1%	35	<1%
Supervised Probation	2,771	62%	3,978	63%
Unsupervised Probation	258	6%	562	9%
Fine	656	15%	1,070	17%
Conditional Discharge	309	7%	1,302	21%
Absolute Discharge	56	1%	133	2%

* Percentages add up to more than 100 due to multiple sentences per offender

Research studies indicate that Aboriginal offenders are more likely to receive sentences of incarceration than non-Aboriginal offenders (LaPrairie 1996). The data from FVC are consistent with these findings. Convicted Aboriginal offenders (30 percent) are almost twice as likely to go to prison as non-Aboriginal offenders (17 percent). Conversely, when we consider the least serious outcome, conditional discharge, we see that non-Aboriginal offenders are almost three times as likely to get a conditional discharge as an Aboriginal offender.

Disturbingly, when we control for a number of variables involving seriousness of the crime (i.e. prior record and weapon use and seriousness of the charge), we find very little moderation of the effects of ethnicity. Overall, Aboriginal offenders are more likely to get a sentence of incarceration and less likely to receive a conditional discharge. These consistent differences in sentencing by ethnicity raise some troubling questions about ethnic bias in sentencing. However, we are aware that our data do not capture all the facts before the court; in particular, we do not have all the information on mitigating and aggravating factors that were weighed at the time of sentencing. It was suggested by one judge in a private discussion that if a convicted offender has a prior history of incarceration it makes it much more likely that they would receive a sentence of incarceration for subsequent offences. In these cases, if an offender has a history of prior incarceration and recidivism, the sentencing judge would have little confidence that a non-carceral sentence would be appropriate or would afford protection for the victim.

This is, of course, the fabric of systemic discrimination. The dilemma we face here is: where do we begin to address that pattern, and at what cost? It is quite likely that there is consensus among prosecutors and judiciary that, in cases of lesser property crimes and/or first offenses for common assault, a prison sentence is not necessary or desirable. The prevalence of probation sentences in FVC is an indicator of this sentiment. However, when faced with a violent offender with a record of violent offences, the safety of the victim becomes a very significant consideration in sentencing. As Amnesty International stated, "societal indifference to the welfare and safety of Indigenous women will allow the perpetrators to escape justice" (*Stolen Sisters*, 2004, p. 1) and it is not unreasonable to conclude that this will fuel greater violence against them.

Final Thoughts

While we are far from conclusions on this issue, I offer some final observations. Our courts and our communities are facing serious challenges regarding sentencing in family violence cases involving Aboriginal offenders. There are some recent innovations in Canada that may provide models for us in the future, for example, the Yukon Family Violence Court and the Homefront Project in Calgary (Statistics Canada, 2003). However, the over-representation of Aboriginal people in Canadian prisons will likely take major systemic changes to overcome. It will require changes to many institutions, in addition to the justice system, to increase the education, employment and socio-economic status of Aboriginal people. In the meantime, Aboriginal women are at very high risk of experiencing violence and abuse.

To respond to the demand by Amnesty International, that an adequate standard to protection be available to Aboriginal women, we need to advocate for proper policing, even when this demand sets up a whole troublesome dynamic in the courts. The case in favour of zero tolerance or pro-arrest policies is primarily a case for protection. There is no other service in our community that has all the components for providing protection in high risk situations:

- 24 hour, 7-days-a-week service
- a rapid response system
- a response unit trained in high risk intervention
- a response that ensures separation of victim and accused with restraining orders if the accused is released
- response without prejudice (no discretion)

The above components exist only among police forces, and the zero tolerance policy is the Winnipeg police service's attempt to ensure that all five components are operating when a person at risk calls the police. In many ways this is cold comfort to those who want true equality extended to Aboriginal women, and, at best, it is only a partial response to the demands of Amnesty International that Canadian authorities protect the rights of Indigenous women. Personal security, a freedom from violence and abuse, is the most basic right of all individuals, and at this stage in history, this freedom is not available to a large percentage of Aboriginal women in Canada.

Notes

1   In Winnipeg Family Violence Court the overwhelming majority of assailants of Aboriginal women are Aboriginal men.

2   Cases are considered family violence matters if the victim is in a relationship with the accused which involves "trust, dependency and /or kinship." Thus, the FVC hears matters of child abuse, spouse abuse, elder abuse, and other family assaults. The category "other family assaults" involve abuse among adult siblings, nieces, nephews, uncles and aunts, etc.

Our identification of an accused or victim's ethnic status results from a composite of information provided in the police and Crown files. Individuals are considered Aboriginal if they have self-disclosed or if their ethnic status is identified in police or Crown files. In the category "Aboriginal origin," we include persons identified as status and non-status Aboriginal as well as Metis. This is a broad category and the determination of entry into this category is dependent upon self or police or Crown identification. Therefore, it is not a precise category. However, given the choice of this determination of ethnicity or no determination at all, we felt it was best to proceed with the available information. Our categories for ethnicity include European origin, Aboriginal origin and Other. The "other" category includes other visible minorities, who, for the purposes of this report, are included in the broad category non-Aboriginal. Finally, because this is an accused-based data set, our most detailed information is on the accused. While we often have information on the ethnicity of the victim, it is not recorded as frequently as the accused's ethnic status.

3   In the eight-year period of data collection we had information on ethnicity for 96 percent of the individuals arrested.

CHAPTER SEVEN

Femicide In Saskatchewan

Deb Farden

Introduction

I wish to begin by acknowledging the values and life events that have shaped this research. It reflects my experiences as a counsellor for women who experienced violence in intimate adult relationships. It also reflects my feminism, my faith in my Creator, and my pervasive belief in non-violent methods of problem solving and peacemaking.

On December 3, 1986, a woman with whom I had had a counselling relationship was murdered by a person or persons then unknown. She was killed three days after leaving the women's shelter at which I worked. All of us at the shelter were devastated and shocked by her murder. We began to examine everything we had done to see if we had overlooked anything that may have prevented this horrible tragedy. As I had worked quite closely with this woman (she had written a poem in my honour), I felt a special sense of both responsibility and loss. In February 1990, I was subpoenaed to testify at the trial of her killer — a man alleged to have been hired by her husband. The defence hoped to use me to discredit her. I felt sickened that what I knew might be used in that way. I never forgot this woman, or the manner of her death. Because of her murder I developed an interest in exploring how the killing of women by intimate partners could be prevented. When I returned to university to complete my master's degree, I embarked on a journey of studying female homicides in this province.

The resulting project was a review of 40 Saskatchewan femicides from 1988 through 1992, described in police documents made available through an agreement with the Department of Justice. The process was an onerous and, at times, overwhelming experience. Often, after a day of reading these files, I would leave angry and with images of violent death in my head. Some of these images still haunt me. This is most true of those femicides that I felt were preventable. In my head I hear these women's unacknowledged pleas for help, pleas that may have been heard but were ignored. I see their dead, violated bodies. A good deal of my anger arose from the fact that rarely was the violent incident in which they were murdered the first act of violence against them by their killers. Too often, neighbours or relatives of the victim or the killer knew about the violence and did nothing. Typically, the killing of these women was extremely brutal and took place over a prolonged period of time, sometimes for days. Rarely were the killings the crimes of passion they were portrayed to be; rather, they were the culmination of years of violence by one man against one woman.

In this article, I make visible the intimate and domestic character of femicide by remembering those women killed by intimate male partners, and I hope to contribute to policies of prevention in the future by describing characteristics of the victims, the killers and the killings.

Research Methods

I use the term *femicide* in its broadest sense to describe the killing of a woman by another person (Crawford & Gartner, 1992). This term includes the range of killings from manslaughter to first-degree murder but does not include the killing of women in self-defence. The phrase *intimate femicide* describes those women "killed by intimate male partners, that is, legal spouses, common-law spouses, and boyfriends, whether current or estranged" (Crawford & Gartner, 1992, p. 27).

I began my research by reviewing official records on homicide, such as those provided by Statistics Canada, coroners' reports, and police records, as well as newspaper reports covering the murders of Saskatchewan women. Information on available sources was recorded on a collection form replicating the one developed by Crawford and Gartner (1992) in their study of intimate femicide in Ontario. With this form, "as many as 49 different characteristics of the victim, her killer, their relationship, the circumstances surrounding the crime, and the legal response to the crime could be recorded" (p. 17).

Official sources, however, were problematic in that they reported the tasks of determining the cause of death, determining the method of the killing, gathering evidence, and reconstructing the crime in order to solve it, whereas my goal was to reflect the perspective of the victim and to examine the possibility of prevention.

Based on information from the Coroners Branch, I compiled a list of 36 women, by date and jurisdiction of death, aged 15 and over, whose deaths were classified as homicides during the period of 1988 through 1992. Four additional femicides came to light through newspaper searches and police-record searches. All known deaths are recorded by the Coroners Branch, which determines the causes of all deaths and classifies them as murder, accident, suicide, or natural cause. Coroners' reports also include medical information on the condition of the body (e.g. medical evidence of previous violence and/or suicide attempts) and provide details as to how these women were killed. What the coroners' records do not tell us is about those women whose deaths are misclassified as accident or suicide when they are actually intimate femicides. Neither do they record the deaths of women who are classified as missing persons but who were actually murdered by an intimate partner. It is, therefore, quite possible that the numbers of femicides and intimate femicides are significantly higher than those discussed in this study.

Findings

My research of the available documents indicated that as many as ten femicides could have been preventable. In addition, two women who survived an attempted intimate femicide were interviewed at length about their experiences. These interviews further reinforce the importance of developing active prevention policies based on reviewing women's stories and women's experiences of violence.

Characteristics of the Victims

Women in common-law relationships were more likely than separated or married women to be killed by intimate partners; single women were more likely than married women to be killed outdoors by strangers. These outdoor killings were more likely to be sexually motivated and to involve sexual assault of the victim. Women of all ages were equally at risk for intimate femicide; however, young women were more likely to be victims of non-intimate femicide. Aboriginal women were killed at a higher rate than white women (24 of 40 cases or 60 percent) yet Aboriginal women make up only 15 percent of the population. They were as likely to be killed in a non-intimate as an intimate femicide (11 to 12 or 50 percent of cases), while white women were killed predominantly through intimate femicide (11 of 16 cases or 69 percent). Another disturbing finding was that the killings of Aboriginal women were less likely to be reported in *The StarPhoenix*. Seven Aboriginal women's killings were not reported compared to one white woman's killing not reported.

Characteristics of the Killers

Most killers had criminal records (27 of 35) and had used alcohol or drugs (26 of 35) at the time they committed the murders. Men who killed current or former wives, girlfriends or lovers were usually convicted of manslaughter (13 of 23 cases or 57 percent), whereas men who killed women not intimate with them were more often convicted of second-degree murder (9 of 17 cases or 53 percent). Men under 35 committed all solved non-intimate femicides in this study. Three cases remained unsolved, but evidence pointed to non-intimate femicide so I classified these killings as such.

The killer was known to have been previously violent towards the victim in nearly two-thirds of intimate femicides, and there had been previous police involvement in almost half the murders. The motives for these killings were usually a man's actual or feared separation from his partner or a disruption of his dominance in the relationship. Men of all ages committed intimate femicide.

Characteristics of the Killings

Stabbings (18) and beatings (10) were the most common methods of killing. Men who used firearms to kill (5) used them exclusively to kill intimate partners. Overkill/multiple methods occurred more often when the murder was intimate femicide. Overkill involves using enough violence to kill someone more than once and may involve the use of multiple methods (i.e. beating and stabbing). Typically, women murdered by intimate partners were killed in their own homes, while non-intimate femicides were more likely to occur outdoors.

Ten Deaths: Were They Preventable?

Upon reviewing the files, I classified 9 of 23 intimate femicides (39 percent) and one of 17 non-intimate femicides (6 percent) as preventable. I will briefly describe each of these incidents in an attempt to honour each woman, her life, and her death. I also recount these stories in the hope that public policy aimed at preventing intimate femicide will be made more effective and that members of the community will be moved to act on behalf of women who are assaulted.

1. Two times in the same night, a victim of intimate femicide told two different cab drivers that she thought her common-law partner was going to kill her that night. One cab driver offered to take her to the police station but she refused; the other cab driver thought "it was just the booze talking." Neither driver registered his information with the police prior to the killing.

2. At least three and possibly more residents of the apartment block in which another victim lived heard the sounds of an assault that continued for hours. One person knocked on the door and complained of the noise, but the assault continued. Another person became so upset at the sounds of the assault that she left the apartment building and did not return for many hours. Some witnesses heard the man threatening to kill the woman, her screams for help, and the sounds of her body hitting the floor and wall. No one called the police.

3. A third woman had had a previous relationship with a man who was under mandatory supervision for manslaughter. He was granted parole in June 1984. In August 1984, she anonymously requested that his parole be revoked as she was afraid of him, but there is no indication that anything came of her request. She was too afraid

of him to stand up to him and to ask him to leave. She had been severely assaulted by him on many occasions and choked to unconsciousness. In the assault that ended her life, there were auditory witnesses to the assault who failed to call the police.

4. A woman in a small community was shot to death by her husband, after an urban police force failed to relay quickly an order to arrest her husband because of his threats to kill her. In this instance, police error appeared to play a large role. On June 9, the woman submitted a statement to police regarding the threats against her, turned over a tape on which her husband threatened to kill her, and described a plan he had to kill her that had been thwarted by other events. Police planned to arrest him and to confiscate his guns but could not locate him and the children who had been abducted. According to a June 10 urban police entry, the police sent a dispatch to the local RCMP advising them to arrest and hold the woman's husband. The RCMP were also informed that a warrant would be issued as soon as possible. According to a June 11 urban police entry, the woman's husband was on their system and a warrant had been issued for his arrest. This was inconsistent with information from the rural community. On June 14, the husband turned the children over to the local RCMP detachment and an officer of the Department of Social Services. He was given a July date to attend court and allowed to go free. His guns were not confiscated; he was not held for psychiatric evaluation. Later that same day, the husband was spotted by another RCMP officer. Because the officer had heard the man was wanted by an urban police force, he ran a Criminal Police Information Centre (CPIC) check on him; however, the check did not indicate that the man was wanted by anyone. The officer did not pick him up. A copy of the tape containing the threats against the woman and warrant information on charges of abduction arrived on June 15, the next day.

Meanwhile, the woman was informed by the Department of Social Services that her children were in the care of the Department, and she made arrangements to get them on June 20. Neither she nor Social Services informed the police or the RCMP that she was going to get her children. Her ex-husband killed her the day she went to pick them up.

5. An RCMP officer accompanied a woman to her farm home to retrieve some property after the completion of the divorce and property settlement. The woman's lawyer expressed grave concern to police and to the woman about her safety. Because she was afraid of her estranged husband's reaction if she arrived with the police, the woman requested the officer remain at the end of the driveway. The officer agreed to her request even though he was there to ensure her safety. He made a phone call and turned the car around. His windows were closed and he failed to hear the gunshots that killed her.

6. Three people across the alley from a house saw what appeared to be a man having sex with a woman who was unconscious or dead. Because they were not certain it was an assault, they decided it was none of their business and did not report the incident to the police. The woman was brutally assaulted and tortured over two days and was still alive when they saw her. She was stabbed and cut with a knife 121 times. Another neighbour heard what sounded like a fight coming from the house but did not call police.

7. An elderly man, who by all accounts had never before been violent, began to have sudden and alarming thoughts of violence, which he reported to a psychiatrist whom he saw three times over a six-week period. The psychiatrist did not take his fears seriously. The man eventually killed his wife.

8. In another case, warning signals accumulated for a year prior to the killing: the man attempted suicide twice, repeatedly spoke of suicide, and on a number of different occasions said he would like to kill himself but that he would kill his wife too because he loved her and did not want to be without her in the afterlife. He stated this about three times at the house party at which he later killed her. No one called police.

9. At least seven or more people on a reserve saw a woman being severely assaulted by her husband over a period of hours. One man tried to intervene but was also assaulted. The woman pounded on people's doors pleading to be let in. None of them opened their door. Witnesses to the assault stated they were too afraid of reprisals from the assaulting man's family either to take the woman in or to call police.

10. Members of an immigrant community became aware that one of
    their members was experiencing increasing paranoia about his food
    being poisoned and people following him and spraying poisons on
    him. They referred him for treatment but he refused medication
    because he believed the pharmacist was poisoning his medication.
    Meanwhile, the man was picked up by police twice for knocking on
    people's doors at night, and taken to hospital for a psychiatric eval-
    uation. Even though he was found in the X-ray room of the hospital
    with a knife, he was released. Three days before he murdered, two
    members of the religious community to which he belonged (one a
    psychiatrist) had an argument over whether or not to certify him.
    The psychiatrist felt they should wait and made plans for the man to
    be returned to his home country the next Saturday. That Friday, he
    murdered a woman who touched his food in a grocery store.

Discussion

Six of these ten murders represent failures of the community. Members
of the communities in which four women lived (cases 2, 3, 6, 9) failed to
report the fatal assaults to the police. Members of the community failed
to report a woman's expressed fears that her partner would kill her (case 1).
Neither did they report one man's expressed intention to kill both himself
and his partner (case 8).

Similar failures are noted by the judicial system. According to Mahon
(1995), a case study in Nova Scotia revealed that, unless a man was charged
for assaulting a woman, related charges were not linked to a pattern of relationship violence. For example, charges such as damage to property (usually
hers), threats to kill, or stalking, were rarely connected to or seen as a part of
a man's pattern of violence against his partner. As a result, police tended to
modify their response, and probation officers failed to adequately consider
the safety of the woman in their interventions. According to Mahon, probation officers often did not know that the offence they were dealing with (i.e.,
damage to property) was related to violence against an intimate partner. In
addition, police officers and prosecutors exercised considerable discretion in
laying charges when the assault involved a "domestic" dispute. This fits with
contentions by feminists that "the powerful institutions of patriarchal society,

namely, the law, the judiciary, the police and the media have largely denied the existence [and the ongoing threat] of femicide" (Radford, 1992, p. 351).

In Saskatchewan's experience of femicide, one woman was murdered by her intimate partner when communication between two police forces failed to quickly and clearly relay instructions to arrest, detain, and charge her estranged husband. Another woman was killed when the police officer who accompanied her to the marital home failed to keep her within earshot and eyesight, even though he was with her specifically to prevent an assault. In case five above, the officer likely experienced a conflict between two police practices — 1) to accompany women in battering situations to their homes solely to prevent an assault, and 2) to work with abused women in a way that is respectful of them. In at least two intimate femicides, neither the women nor the communities in which they lived believed either the police or the judicial system could keep them safe. In case three described above, the woman had anonymously asked the Parole Board for protection from a man who had previously committed manslaughter, but there was no indication that the Parole Board responded. In case nine, the killer and his family terrorized the entire community, which did not report the fatal assault to the police for four days. Based on previous reports to police about this family, members of the community did not believethe police could protect them from violence by the killer and his family. Reporting to police had made it worse. In both these killings, the women experienced the dual failure of their communities and an arm of the judicial system.

One intimate and one non-intimate femicide can be attributed to the failure of the medical community to accurately assess the dangerous mental state of the killer. Both killers reported severe psychiatric symptoms. In case seven described above, the killer had reported the sudden onset of recurring, persistent thoughts of violence and asked his doctor to stop him before he hurt someone; in case 10, the killer had reported extreme paranoia and doctors had verified previous violence by him when he was in this mental state. Both times doctors made decisions allowing the killers to continue living in the community.

Notably, of ten preventable killings, nine were intimate femicides. How is it that what happens in the family is deemed by society to be a private affair to the extent that individuals fail to intervene when an event as serious as an assault occurs?

Preventive Themes from Interviews:
Rena & Marilyn, Two Women Who Survived

Marilyn related the following dream shortly after we completed our first interview together. She had been consumed with memories of her former relationship and was concerned that her participation might help prevent other women from experiencing what she did.

> I dreamt about a woman that I've known since childhood, and I know that she . . . has been abused all the years that she has been married. I dreamt that she called me and said, "Marilyn, come to my house. I'm leaving John, and I want as many people here as possible when I tell him and when I leave." I went right over there and there were about five or six of us there to get her safely out of the house. And I thought, this is one weird dream, you know. But obviously the whole thing of abuse has been on my mind a lot lately, and it takes those five or six other people to get a woman safely out.

In the process of designing this research to focus on the prevention of intimate femicide, I realized that vital information may come from women who had survived attempted murder by intimate partners. Therefore, I conducted in-depth interviews with two women (Rena and Marilyn) who had survived attempted murder by their husbands. I looked at themes of prevention within the femicidal attempts themselves and within the entire context of the stories as the women chose to tell them. Both Rena and Mark and Marilyn and Mel had been in marriages longer than ten years when the attempts on the women's lives were made.

Both interviews took place ten years after the attempts on their lives. Rena had never told her story to anyone. Marilyn had told her story twice before, but she had never talked about the marital rapes she experienced. Neither woman had ever seen a written account of the attacks on their lives. Both reported difficulty at seeing their stories in print and declined to read the transcripts of our interviews or the shortened, edited versions of their stories. They did not check for accuracy of content. Both said they just could not do it.

Common themes about prevention emerged from these interviews, centring on systemic issues of a number of social institutions — the judicial, the religious, the medical, the family, and the community. All these levels of society play a role in what Pence (1988) has named community collusion in the perpetuation of male violence against women in intimate relationships.

The Judicial System

The judicial system colluded in the violence against Rena and Marilyn in many ways. Mark was never arrested, even though he had breached his restraining order (threatened to kill Rena, one of their children, and her parents), and admitted to a witness that he had tried to kill her. The attempt on her life began a campaign of terror against Rena that continues, in a somewhat muted fashion, to this day: "Because he will still stalk me, and he will stalk the kids, and he never lets go of anything." At the time of Rena's initial contact with the police system, there were no zero tolerance policies in place; however, according to Ursel (2002), even when policies are in place, individual officers fail to act on them.

Mel tried to kill Marilyn the day after he was served with a restraining order from her lawyer's office. Previously, Marilyn had had charges filed against Mel, but his violence against her continued unabated. This worked to create an unwillingness on her part to press charges against Mel after this last, near-fatal assault. She believed Mel would kill her when he was released from jail if the RCMP proceeded with a charge of attempted murder against him. Marilyn believed her best chance lay in dropping all criminal action. The RCMP officer who investigated her attempted murder collaborated with her in making this decision. As it does for many women, a dilemma existed for Marilyn and the state. Even when charges were laid, the judicial process moved exceedingly slowly in its confrontation of the violent man with whom Marilyn had lived — so slowly that she gave up on it. As Light and Rivkin (1994) have commented, the system itself inhibits women from seeking justice:

> Until women agree that criminal justice system intervention is the most appropriate option for them, or until they believe that the system can provide them with greater ongoing safety than they can attain

through nonintervention, many will continue to seek police protection to stop the immediate violence but will not support the laying of charges (p. 17).

Indeed, the laying of charges can actually increase the risk of femicide. According to Marilyn, this happened to her. Her husband had lost her, his wife; he had rape and assault charges pending against him, and he felt he had nothing left to lose by murdering her. Neither survivor believed the judicial system could, then or now, provide protection from violent partners.

The Medical System

While Rena's primary contact with helpers, after her attempted murder, was supportive, Marilyn was not so fortunate. The medical system colluded in the violence against her when medical personnel failed to consider Marilyn's battery by Mel as a life-threatening condition, and did not attempt to ascertain or secure her safety. Over the years Marilyn had seen many doctors about symptoms directly related to Mel's violence against her (i.e. bruises) and ones that were indirectly related (vague aches and pains). Even when informed about Mel's assaults against her, doctors failed to make her safety a primary focus of treatment. The focus was on helping Mel get better — on Mel's headaches, on Mel's childhood, and on Mel's bipolar illness. In terms of the femicidal assault itself, medical personnel, after being told by Mel that he had just tried to kill his wife, left her alone with and responsible for Mel. They did not ask Marilyn what had happened nor did they examine her. They did not talk to her apart from Mel. They did not admit him to hospital. Instead they told her she had to drive him to another hospital in another community (more than an hour away) because there were no beds. Her experience is consistent with Warshaw's research findings. Warshaw (1989) "examined the medical records of encounters between medical staff (nurses and physicians) and women whose injuries were highly indicative of having been caused by abuse." She describes medical encounters in which "what is most significant is not seen" and in which a woman's initial attempts to disclose the violence were not attended to: "Together, the doctor, nurse, and patient construct a medical history ... that extracts an event ... from its status as an event" (p. 513). The battered woman is reduced to medical symptoms describing the impact of his violence on her body parts but in which it is never said that it was her boyfriend's fist that caused her "blunt face trauma." In Marilyn's case, no one examined her for trauma or even asked her if anything had happened to her, even though Mel had said he wanted to kill her. Therapists and counsellors have played a similar role in rendering violence against women invisible. In their offices, "it is never spoken that a crime has been committed, much less that he has committed it" (Kaufman, 1992, p. 239).

Community Factors

According to both Rena and Marilyn, individuals in their communities affected their safety in a number of ways. Some individuals in both their communities chose not to see physical evidence (i.e., bruises) of the violence against them; however, Marilyn began to find her way out of her violent marriage when a neighbour acknowledged that he knew Mel was hitting her. This neighbour's presence saved her from some assaults because Mel would never hit her in front of anyone. Marilyn stated that when someone outside the marital home knew about the violence, the terrible power of secret shame began to break down. Her neighbour did not blame her and she began to develop a support network that helped her to change her opinions about herself. In spite of herself, she had begun to believe she was as worthless as Mel said she was. Marilyn's statement is consistent with findings by Carlson et al. (2003) that being a victim of abuse increases women's experience of depression and anxiety. Through supportive others she came to believe in her own worth, to develop a sense of competency, and to believe that she had the right to a life without violence. "This was the beginning of the end" (Marilyn, 1996).

No one acknowledged knowing about Mark's violence against Rena before their separation. People had occasionally asked her about bruises but she shrugged it off. Her husband was a well-respected, wealthy businessman from a good family. Their public appearance was so discrepant with their private lives that Rena did not think people would believe her and so, when she left Mark, she moved to a new community. Despite lack of validation and acknowledgement, by moving, Rena was able to find a way to make herself safe. She undertook the momentous task of deconstructing her life as a married woman in a community that supported her abusive spouse, and of reconstructing her entire life — home, community, work, church, school, and friends.

Rena and Marilyn both described being helped by people in their communities after their separations — friends who gave emotional support, neighbours who watched their homes and reported when they saw anyone lurking around, people who checked on them and who agreed to call the police if they heard something disturbing. These experiences were in direct contrast to the isolation they had experienced while they lived with assaultive husbands. This isolation from their community had enabled their husbands' violence to go unchallenged. The only person Marilyn had been able to contact without fear was her doctor. Doctors, therefore, were in a unique position to help, but did not.

Family and Religious Factors

Marilyn's and Rena's families and churches both colluded in the violence in a less immediate way. Both women stated that their families and churches were primary players in their socialization into the acceptance of patriarchy as a right. Both women's families and churches believed that the man was the head of the house and trained them to accept male authority to the extent that Marilyn and Rena were left questioning themselves when that male authority was abusive.

Although both women reported growing up in non-violent homes, they both stated that they believed the patriarchal structures of their families and churches helped set them up to enter into, and to stay in, abusive relationships. They were taught that women were to submit to men, and if that man was abusive they believed it reflected on them as women. Both family and church supported the idea that the man was the head of the house. These beliefs affected their decision to stay with abusive mates. Both women also stated that they did not believe they could count on help from the churches they attended throughout their abusive relationships, because they felt they had failed as Christian women and perceived a lack of support from the church community. In addition to the collusion of family and church, abused women often face additional barriers concerning church and family. Abusive men frequently denigrate their partners' deeply held beliefs and use threats against their families and loved ones as additional vehicles of control. Both Marilyn and Rena reported that their husbands used their families against them. Mel had "promised" to kill Marilyn's family should she leave or tell about his violence. Similarly, after Rena's separation, Mark threatened to kill Rena's parents and one of her children. In research published in 2002, Riger found that "violence against women had serious ramifications for those in her support system, particularly for her extended family" (p. 198), as they experienced acts and or threats of violence against them or their property.

Integration of Findings

Why do police so often fail to intervene in "domestic" disputes? Why do doctors not ask about physical violence when women come in with vague somatic complaints or physical injuries? Why do neighbours and others who witness a "domestic" dispute fail to intervene or call for help? Why is violence against women in the home so often regarded as a private affair in which we do not intervene? Each of these questions points towards community collusion in the perpetuation of violence against women in intimate relationships. Significantly, the women who survived attributed their ability to remain safe and out of the abusive relationships to those in the community who dared to reach out and help and believe them.

The Community

The communities here described are informed by historically established ideologies of the home as private and of women as possessions and subject to men. I recognize that these concepts spring from a Eurocentric perspective that may not adequately address issues of violence in Saskatchewan's Aboriginal communities, whose experiences of colonization and attempted assimilation forever changed how they live. Racism compounds the complexities of femicide and shapes the experiences of women of colour, whose experience of violence is rooted in a history of colonialism and imperialism (Radford, 1992). It is impossible to know from recorded history whether Aboriginal women experienced violence in intimate relationships or if patriarchy operated before First Nations' contact with the Europeans; however, the Aboriginal women in this research were deeply affected by patriarchal and racist beliefs.

Home as Private and Women as Property

The concept of the home as private is central to the inaction of social institutions when violence occurs in families. In this research, even "in the direst of circumstances," individual members of the community refused to breach "the sanctity of the home." Had someone intervened, it is possible that nine women killed by intimate partners would still be alive. Neighbours or other witnesses failed to intervene or call police because they regarded violence towards an intimate female partner as "none of their business" (neighbours across the back alley case) or they regarded verbal threats to kill as "blowing off steam" (cab driver case). Both women survivors talked about meeting people who chose not to see and not to know about the violence against them by accepting lame excuses for their bruises. These people did not want to believe that "upstanding" members of the community would beat their wives.

According to Daly and Wilson (1992), women are at the greatest risk of intimate femicide when they initiate separation and divorce. That was certainly true for the women in this research, who were killed when they tried to end the relationship. Others were killed when they questioned their partner's actions or behaviour, or refused his requests. The attempted murders of both survivors occurred after they left their violent partners. The women were not allowed to stand as equals with their male partners. Bean (1992), who wrote a book on women murdered by men they loved, notes, "Men continue to feel entitled to, and responsible for, the control of their wives' personal assets, including money that women either earn or bring to the relationship" (p. 19). A woman's decision-making power, even over her own money, is often subject to his review. "He feels entitled to do this. Nor does she see anything extraordinary about what he does" (p. 20). One of the women in this study was killed after refusing to give her partner money. She had borrowed money from her father to pay off debts her partner had incurred on their behalf but without her consent. When she refused to give her partner control of her money, he murdered her.

Perceptions of the home as private, and of matters between spouses as nobody's business, may contribute to systematic non-intervention when women are at risk of intimate male violence. Prevention is deterred when people are reluctant to intervene in "domestic disputes." The same is not true of non-intimate male violence. In fact, intervention is more likely to occur when others regard the assailant as a stranger.

Historic Legitimacy of Women as Property and Subject to Men

There is some indication that violence toward women has been legitimized by historical practice. According to Ellen Pence (1984), "in this century wife beating was the legal right of a husband. It was a clearly legitimate way for a man to assert his legal and presumed moral authority over his wife" (p. 478). As late as the 1970s, adultery by a woman was considered a justifiable reason under the law for the committal of intimate femicide. "Killing rage," in response to his wife's adultery was considered the act of a "reasonable man," but the reverse was never true. Daly & Wilson (1988, 1992) attribute this behaviour to the concept of "male sexual proprietariness" — the tendency of men to think of women as sexual and reproductive property. Intimate femicides are often precipitated by a man's suspicion or knowledge of his partner's infidelity, by a man's knowledge or fear of the woman's leaving, or by a man's perception of the woman's real or imagined rejection of him in some way. Several of the women in this research were murdered by intimate males for real or imagined affairs; eight were murdered over separation or suspicions of separation from their partner. Another eight women were murdered for "going against" their partners in some way. Campbell (1992, in Radford & Russell) refers to the killing of women "going against" their partners as murders related to male dominance issues. Within the violent relationship itself, notions of male dominance and of woman as property may contribute to violence against women. Social constructions of male dominance might affect responses of individuals within the community and interventions by judicial or medical institutions.

Discussion and Recommendations

In this research, the women at greatest risk for intimate femicide were not employed outside the home, were between 26 and 30 years old, and lived with an unemployed male with a criminal record. There were more likely to be witnesses to her killing than in non-intimate femicides, and these witnesses were less likely to call police than witnesses to assaults by strangers. Aboriginal women were equally at risk for both intimate and non-intimate femicide; however, white women were primarily at risk for intimate femicide. After reviewing these files, I would suggest that nine of the 23 intimate and one of 17 non-intimate femicides could likely have been prevented, and, accordingly, I offer the following recommendations aimed at preventing femicide in Saskatchewan.

Recommendations for Public Policy

1. Witnesses (auditory or visual) to domestic assault should report all assaults to police or face criminal charges. Perhaps, if it is found that a person or persons observed or heard a domestic assault and did not report, they could be charged. In this study, four women were killed after adult witnesses failed to report an assault in progress.

2. Police should regard reporting of intimate assaults by women as evidence of possible lethal relationships. In 43 percent of intimate femicides, there had been prior police involvement.

3. Communication links within and between police forces should be improved, as communication failure directly contributed to the death of one woman.

4. Police and other members of the judicial system need to take a woman-centered approach to women's safety. They need to collaborate with abused women regarding their safety and to discuss with them the limitations of the law in providing them with safety. In the only incidence in which a woman reported positive police contact, the officer had collaborated with her regarding her need for safety.

5. Advocates for victims, counsellors, police, and the medical community need to work intensively with women at risk for femicide to help them mobilize a community response which can help keep them safe. Both women who survived an attempted intimate femicide reported that their community (i.e., neighbours, friends, etc.) helped keep them safe.

6. Nearly two-thirds of the killers were under the age of 35. A more concerted effort must be made to educate young men, adolescents, and boys about the risks of violent behavior and to work at changing cultural beliefs that allow violence against women to go unchecked. Education must occur formally and informally, as social institutions currently collude in the violence.

7. Any fears of being killed expressed by women in violent relationships must be taken seriously by parole boards, police, judges, lawyers, health professionals, and the general public. Some women who were later murdered by partners had expressed their concerns to a parole board, doctors or nurses, police, lawyers, friends, and taxi drivers. Inaction or inadequate follow-up was the most frequently noted response by all of the above. Perhaps it is time to treat jokes about killing wives in the same way as jokes about blowing up airplanes — the utterer of the threat has to prove there was no ill intent and that he is not a danger to his female partner.

8. A high prevalence of a criminal record amongst perpetrators of intimate femicide suggests a need to consider any charges as an indication of possible relationship violence. An even stronger connection to relationship violence needs to be made when the charges, often not specifically charges of partner assault, are none the less connected to his pattern of violence against her. Charges such as disturbing the peace, destruction of property, and threats to kill must go further and state that the perpetrator was disturbing the peace of his ex-partner, destroying the property of his partner or estranged partner, or threatening to kill his wife or her family. Later charges need to reflect past infractions against the same person. Without this link in place, probation officers may be unaware that the offender has a history of relationship violence and may fail to consider partner assault in making plans to rehabilitate an offender.

9. Parole boards need a mechanism to look at anonymous requests, particularly when that request comes from an intimate partner. Intimate partners are the most likely to be in danger from someone who has previously been incarcerated.

In addition to these recommendations, anecdotal data suggest that sometimes abusive men delay separation/divorce actions in order to maintain control of women who are attempting to leave. Therefore, the legal system needs to tighten up unreasonable delays in its system. These delays prolong the period of dangerous contact, as each legal step towards separation escalates the risk to the women who are leaving.

What is the political significance of femicide? According to Radford (1992), femicide is a form of capital punishment that affects victims, families, friends, and, most importantly, women as a group. Every publicized rape by a stranger reminds women they are not safe in public spaces. Every story of a woman murdered by an intimate male partner or ex-partner reminds women that they are not safe in private spaces, or that they are "lucky" because their man is not violent. These murders, however, were not inevitable. They may have been prevented with help from the community, from medical professionals, or from various arms of the judicial system.

CHAPTER EIGHT

Helping the Helpers:
Exploring Solutions to Secondary Traumatic Stress

Stephanie L. Martin

Purpose

The intent of this project is to explore female, front-line anti-violence service providers' experiences of secondary traumatic stress and coping, with a specific focus on the solutions or strategies they implement in their daily personal and professional roles to counter the potential "costs of caring." The results of this investigation contribute to the developing conceptual understanding of the impact and treatment of secondary traumatic stress, and inform enhanced preventative intervention with potentially vulnerable helpers. The Canadian Research Institute for the Advancement of Women is gratefully acknowledged for their support of this project.

Review

Although secondary traumatic stress — also referred to as vicarious trauma, compassion fatigue, and secondary victimization — is well recognized by those who work in the area of traumatology, it has only recently been conceptualized for research and intervention purposes (Arvay 2001; Figley, 2002; Stamm, 1999). In particular, research has begun to demonstrate that while many helpers find satisfaction in helping people who experience extremely stressful events, secondary exposure to traumatic stress can have a negative impact on helpers and those they seek to help (Stamm, 1999).

The concept of secondary traumatic stress is based on the premise that the repetitive, cumulative effects of others' stories of trauma can become highly invasive and deregulating for the care provider (Richardson, 2001; Stamm, 1999). Symptomatically, secondary traumatic stress is nearly identical to post-traumatic stress disorder (Diagnostic and Statistical Manual of Mental Disorders, 4th Ed., APA, 2000), except that it applies to those emotionally affected by the trauma of another, and is also related to interpersonal perceptions and morale. Classic symptoms for the care provider may include acute intrusive images, nightmares, emotional numbing, dissociative experiences, and an exaggerated startle response. However, current literature also suggests that the effects of secondary traumatic stress are cumulative and permanent, and have a severe impact on both personal and professional life (Saakvitne & Pearlman, 1996). Hence, additional effects may include changes in how an individual experiences self and others, such as changes in feelings of safety, increased cynicism and disconnection from loved ones. Left unaddressed, secondary traumatic stress in helpers may also lead to depression and increased use of drugs and/or alcohol. Secondary traumatic stress has also been associated with higher rates of physical illness, greater use of sick leave, higher turnover, lower morale, lower productivity and decreased clinical judgment, which may result in client care/service delivery errors.

In his review, Figley (2002) recommends that research in the area of secondary traumatic stress needs to move in the direction of focusing on incidence and prevalence, as well as prevention and intervention in unique populations of potentially vulnerable helpers. Figley (2002) is concerned with determining who is most vulnerable to compassion fatigue, and what type of work settings and associated conditions set the foundation for a helper's vulnerability to secondary traumatic stress.

While all helping professionals are vulnerable to compassion fatigue (Berger, 2001), front-line crisis counsellors for abused women may be particularly vulnerable (Arvay, 2001). Acute incidents of violence and the chronic, devastating reality of persistent woman abuse in society (Brzozowski, 2004) may negatively affect front-line helpers of abused women whose efforts to assist may, at times, seem in vain. Furthermore, Richardson

(2001) indicates that the collective efforts of anti-violence workers are not always recognized and rewarded by society, and that a comprehensive understanding of the necessity and importance of anti-violence work, as well as the difficult environments in which the work takes place, requires further development.

Ultimately, because both the care provider and the consumer suffer when the helper's distress or impairment is inadequately addressed (Meldrum, King & Spooner, 2002; O'Conner, 2001), hurting helpers may inadvertently hinder our progress towards finding solutions to violence and abuse on a broader societal level. It is also of significant concern that women represent the vast majority of care providers of abused women, which renders the research question one of significant interest to the social, political and economic welfare of women in Canada.

Methodology

Approach

This research is grounded in feminist philosophy, which emphasizes the relevance and importance of women's diverse perspectives as well as their appropriate collaborative participation in the research enterprise (Kimmer & Crawford, 1999; Morris, 2002). Both quantitative measures and a qualitative research interview were employed to gather data on the extent of reported indicators of and potential solutions for secondary traumatic stress. Quantitative results yielded basic descriptive information, designed to assist in contextualizing participants' accounts of their experience with secondary traumatic stress and coping. Participants' verbatim accounts are embedded throughout the text to illustrate core themes relating to front-line anti-violence workers' *experiences* with and *solutions* to secondary traumatic stress (Van Manen, 1990)

Participant recruitment. Participants were recruited via posted advertisements and word-of-mouth. For inclusion, participants were required to be female, front-line anti-violence counsellors for abused women, over the age of 18, and able to commit approximately three hours to the research process. Due to the specialized nature of the participant pool, ethical safeguards required particular and consistent emphasis throughout the research process.

Procedures

Three procedures were used for data collection: 1) a demographic questionnaire provided sample descriptors; 2) two measures — *Brief Symptom Inventory* and *Compassion Satisfaction and Fatigue Subscales-RIII* — yielded quantitative information relating to the incidence and degree of traumatic stress; and, 3) a semi-structured interview provided information relating to the *experience* of and *solutions* to secondary traumatic stress.

Measures

The *Brief Symptom Inventory* is used by human service providers in mental health, medical, and other clinical settings, as well as for research purposes where level of psychological functioning and/or pre- and post-intervention data are of interest (Derogatis, 1993). This measure contains 53 items and takes approximately eight to ten minutes to complete. Although nine primary symptom dimensions are measured, such as anxiety, depression, and somatization, the *Global Severity Index* — designed to provide an overall, temporal measure of psychological functioning — is of interest for the purposes of this project.

The *Compassion Satisfaction/Fatigue Scales* (Figley, 2002) have been developed and modified over the past several years. Although more research is needed to contribute to the psychometric development and standardization of this measure, it was employed primarily as an exploratory tool and general aggregate measure of compassion satisfaction and compassion fatigue for this particular sample. The *Compassion Satisfaction* scales are a measure of the pleasure and satisfaction one derives from being able to be an effective caregiver; the *Compassion Fatigue* subscale is a measure of work-related secondary exposure to extremely stressful events, such as repeatedly hearing stories about the traumatic events in others' lives.

Participant Description

Nineteen female, front-line anti-violence counsellors chose to participate in this study. The participants ranged in age from 27 to 64, and reported a variety of background preparation for their roles as helpers, from college- to Master's-level training. Several participants indicated their Aboriginal ancestry and incorporated traditional healing practices into their work with abused women. Several participants worked part-time in their helping roles, and all reported pursuing continuing education on a regular basis. Some participants have worked in the anti-violence field for several decades, while others were relatively new to the field.

Results

Descriptive Analysis

Psychological functioning. Participants scored an average global severity index (GSI) of 57, compared to an average GSI among non-patient adult females of 49, which indicates an increased rate of psychological distress in this particular participant-sample of front-line anti-violence workers. In addition, individual GSI scores ranging from 33 to 72 suggest a broad range of individual psychological functioning at the time of measurement.

Compassion satisfaction. Participants scored an average of 38 on compassion satisfaction (CS), with individual scores ranging from 20 to 47. A score of 38 suggests an average degree of CS in this particular group of front-line anti-violence workers. According to Stamm (2002), higher CS scores are associated with greater satisfaction with one's ability to caregive, including deriving pleasure from helping, enjoying colleagues, feeling good about one's ability to help, and feeling like one is making a meaningful contribution. Indeed, participants anecdotally confirmed that they receive satisfaction and fulfillment through their front-line anti-violence work with women. Sources of satisfaction related primarily to bearing witness to women's strength and resilience in the face of violence and abuse, celebrating small, positive changes in the way women view themselves and their options, and appreciating the bonding and mutual empowerment that can arise in a therapeutic context. For example, one participant expanded on the reward value of her work:

> The rewarding thing for me is to see these people, these women, who are courageous, strong, and brave, actually take that to a new level, where they feel good about themselves, where they're not giving that away to somebody, they're keeping it for themselves, so that they can better themselves and their children's lives.

Secondary traumatic stress. Participants scored an average of 16 on compassion fatigue (CF), with individual scores ranging from five to 27. A score of 16 suggests a non-concerning degree of CF within this overall sample of front-line anti-violence workers. Higher scores on CF are associated with work-related secondary traumatic stress, often with rapid onset as a result of highly stressful caregiving (Stamm, 2002). As expected, all participants commented on stress resulting from the typical demands of human service work such as chronic understaffing, chronic insecure funding and under-funding, and demanding, often unpredictable, caseloads.

Interestingly, although not indicated by the aggregate CF score, all participants also reported a variety of symptoms consistent with secondary traumatic stress, including indications of altered world view, as well as concerns regarding the general well-being of self and colleagues. Reported symptoms included: physical and mental exhaustion, decreased quality of eating and sleeping, shortness of breath, impatience, irritability, judgmental and/or black-and-white thinking, not wanting to come to work, not wanting to see particular clients, self-doubt regarding skill level and knowledge base, impaired judgment at work and at home, and questions about therapeutic effectiveness and impact, to name only a few. One participant observed a direct relationship between the nature of front-line anti-violence work, her personal coping repertoire, and a variety of symptoms typically reported as being consistent with secondary traumatic stress:

> The symptoms would be agitation, irritability, not sleeping, eating — I would eat comfort foods to calm myself, to take my mind off of the work ... Chronic, chronic sore throat, achy muscles ... Self-doubt, like "maybe I'm no good ..."

Many participants also expanded on behavioural and emotional tendencies consistent with what Baranowsky (2002) refers to as the "silencing response" in counselling/therapeutic contexts. The silencing response consists of tendencies wherein assumptions guide the clinician to shut down, redirect, minimize, or neglect traumatic material within a therapeutic context, and is thought to be of high risk to both helper and client. The following excerpt illustrates this concern:

> I know a lot of workers in this field who give up on the women, and they become the abuser, you know? Telling the women what they should do, and how they should do it. There's a very fine line and, unfortunately, this field can attract people into "helping" who may have power and control issues themselves. I see that a lot. [The helpers] judge why the women go back, or why they leave ... that isn't our place to do that.

Several participants reported examples of altered world view, with both positive and negative outcomes, as well as concerns about personal safety:

> You become aware of the continuum of violence, and what I have found for myself is that I am less willing to tolerate what I used to take in. Professionally, it's given me a really good grounding for what I offer women. Personally, it has made me much more aware and cautious in my own life about what I'm looking for. When you do this work, you come to know that violence is everywhere, that's the downside. Sometimes, I wish I could just set it aside, but I can't go back and not know what I know.

> There's a "cost," in that I'm isolated; there's a "cost," that I know that I feel like I shouldn't have to know these things. It's changed my world view. A few years ago, I was walking in my neighbourhood and someone's plate glass window had been broken; it was obvious that that's what had happened. My mind went to "a woman got thrown through that window;" so, when I see a man buying flowers, I think, "What did he do?" And, sometimes the "cost" is not sleeping well; I will sleep very broken and dream about not necessarily the details per se, but the woman's struggle, and that will get wrapped into my own life, so I have this horrible sleep.

Finally, many participants also reported concern for the well-being of their colleagues, and openly questioned the prospects of enjoying a sense of personal well-being while continuing to work in the anti-violence field. For example:

> I've questioned some of my peers in terms of doing this work and
> staying healthy, as it is such difficult work — I see women smok-
> ing, and I see women who are drinking, and I know women, like
> myself, who are eating, and so I really question, at times, is doing
> this sort of work healthy? Also, though, more recently, I've seen
> women who are doing this work who seem healthy.

Overall, quantitative aggregate results indicate a higher than average
degree of psychological distress, but comparatively normal levels of CS and
CF in this particular sample of front-line anti-violence workers. Of note,
however, is the broad range in individual scores, which suggests variability
in individual symptom reporting and coping styles related to secondary
traumatic stress. Aside from a non-concerning aggregate CF score of 16, all
participants reported personal experiences with secondary traumatic stress
and coping, as well as satisfaction with their direct work with clients.

Thematic Analysis: Balancing the Costs of Caring
From a preventative perspective, it is critical to explore and understand
the potential individual, relational, and organizational solutions that may
counter the cost of caring for vulnerable helpers. Thematic analysis of
solutions to secondary traumatic stress cluster around several areas: education, self-awareness and self-responsibility, self-care, connection, balance,
approach, workplace policy and practice, and systemic issues.

Education. Secondary traumatic stress is ideally approached from a preventative perspective, focusing on educational initiatives throughout training
and practice. Without training in the realm of secondary traumatic
stress, helpers may be reluctant to disclose their distressing experiences,
thereby exacerbating feelings of isolation, shame, and confusion related to
secondary traumatic stress. In terms of training, several participants were
emphatic about how important it is during the early-training years to gain
exposure to the signs and symptoms associated with secondary traumatic
stress, and to understand the potential realities and consequences of a
career as a front-line anti-violence counsellor. As one participant stated:
"Go in with your eyes wide open." Another participant recommends due
caution in committing to a career in the front-line anti-violence field, and

suggests a specific strategy to develop awareness of this particular career path:

> Shadow someone that's been in the field at least for a couple of months before you go full in. I've seen people come into front-line crisis work that are really uncomfortable and uninformed.

Training and personal disposition considerations also appear to be important when compensating the costs of caring over the long term:

> The university could be more vigilant about [practicum] placements, and keep in mind which criteria [are required in a person]. That students are getting adequate supervision for the clinical work they're doing during the first period [of training], and that they're able to take feedback. You need to get regular feedback when you're doing this work.

Finally, several participants also recommend pursuing ongoing education and training as an important tool for remaining informed, inspired and interested in anti-violence work:

> Keep abreast of current research and literature because I think it is empowering to learn new techniques, not to stay stagnant in our approach to helping people.

Self-awareness and self-responsibility. Effective helping requires that helpers develop awareness of personal vulnerabilities to secondary traumatic stress (Figley, 2002; Saakvitne & Pearlman, 1996). In fact, knowing oneself in terms of personal limitations and taking responsibility for one's needs and emotional and physical well-being appears to be a cornerstone to healthy longevity in the anti-violence field. One participant clearly comments on the importance of this theme as it relates to her helping role:

> Know your own biases; know your self! It's powerful to really get to know yourself before you step into a field like this — really important! Some people have avoided that process in their own

personal lives, and that can lead to problems within the counselling relationship.

Furthermore, remaining willing to admit to personal stress, particularly
that which relates to clients' stories of trauma, is important in maintaining
a sense of emotional and physical health while working in a front-line
anti-violence capacity. As indicated, all participants commented on being
affected by their clients' stories. For example, one participant discussed the
tendency to being triggered by clients' stories:

> That doesn't mean I'm ineffective — that's part of what happens
> [in helping others]. But you need to have the awareness in finding
> out what catches you, and then do the work you need to do so it
> doesn't catch you all the time.

Because of this phenomenon, developing constructive responses to
body signals as symptoms of stress is an important resource towards
addressing secondary traumatic stress. Another participant speaks to this
process in action:

> I might get [migraine headaches] twice a year, so I'll know, yeah,
> "cool it, and don't worry so much" ... "Everything's going to be
> okay." I'll increase my smudging and my meditating, and realize
> that what's going to happen is going to happen — some things we
> have power over, and other things we just don't.

Also of critical importance to many of the participants is the concept of
boundaries, particularly as they relate to the therapeutic helping relationship between a front-line worker and an abused woman. For example, one
participant expands on the importance of maintaining a clear sense of the
parameters of her helping role as important to balancing the cost of caring:

> I see people wanting to be people's friends and not really being
> able to differentiate. I have very clear boundaries, even though I
> can share an amount, but I'm very aware of where they are, and
> where their problems stop and I begin.

Finally, the anti-violence field has a high job-turnover rate, with individuals often not remaining in their occupational roles for more than a few years. Participants in this study appear to be an exception to this trend, but many emphasize personal choice regarding occupational trajectory as important to their ongoing commitment to the work:

> I have for myself, almost a checklist that I keep mentally. If I start having really negative feelings about what I'm doing, that's one of my check marks. If I start to get to a space where I'm starting to blame my clients for things that they don't own and having nothing to do with, there's another check mark. Withdrawing from clients, withdrawing from staff. I keep a running tab of when it's time to move out of this area of work.

Self-care. Caring for oneself, in the transformative sense (Pearlman, 1999; Saakvitne & Pearlman, 1996), appears to be an important counterbalance to secondary traumatic stress. Although self-care often conjures up images of simplistic indulgences, such as warm baths and aromatherapy, such activities are critical in terms of recharging helpers and countering the intense empathic disposition required in their roles as helpers. Strategies for self-care vary as much as the personalities of front-line workers, and include such activities as bodily comforts, purposeful journaling, and traditional practices such as massage, yoga, meditation, smudging and cleansing. Importantly, the restorative aspect of self-care lies in one's ability to transcend the particular stressors of anti-violence work, rather than merely approaching self-care as a stress reduction strategy. This participant alludes to the transformative and healing dimensions of self-care:

> Truly understand self-care. Truly get a grasp on what your needs are — heal — begin the process of healing yourself and regain yourself. Make self-care an ongoing process that doesn't stop. The moment that you think you've done all your healing, back away from the work and re-examine that! This line of work is extremely intense at times, so there's a need to heal from that.

Connection. Countering the isolation inherent in anti-violence work is largely achieved through connection with others, including friends, family, colleagues, supervisors/administrators and spiritual figures:

> I have a wonderful partner, and I spend good quality time with him. I derive strength from my family, but I've had to learn how to cultivate these relationships. I need a support system. Why not cultivate two or three or four really good friendships? You don't need anybody that's going to latch on to you and be needy. A good healthy friendship is what we need. Be your own best friend too!

> I have a strong belief in my Creator, and everyday I try and pray and ask him to help me go through my day and to, to be strong for the people I'm working for so that I can help them.

However, several participants commented on the need to exercise due caution regarding disclosure of anti-violence related stress within the context of primary relationships as a means of *protecting* these connections from the potential *contamination* of secondary traumatic stress.

Many participants also emphasized the importance of positive, supportive and constructively challenging collegial relationships as a means of countering the inherent isolation of anti-violence work and as a way of enhancing a sense of personal well-being and expanded meaning in life and work. Some anti-violence workers also indicated that they may benefit from professional counselling or intervention. However, there remains a stigma associated with help-seeking within this particular sample of participants. In particular, participants elaborated on the lack of access to qualified and knowledgeable helpers, as well as the negative judgments that helpers may receive as a result of seeking assistance:

> Finding people who have been in this field for a while who are not burnt out, or damaged by the work — that's a real hard thing! Who do you go to, how will you be judged?

Balance. Balance, in the words of the participants, is imperative to countering the cost of caring. There is a prominent appreciation, in the participants' accounts, of the subjective nature of living in and maintaining a sense of balance:

> Do what you need to do to create balance in your own life, both in your world view and in your life. [The work] demands it, DEMANDS attention to balance, to have ongoing healthy interactions with life and everything. Make sure you eat well, make sure you sleep well. Consider your own needs and don't feel guilty about that!

Balance is also very much about defining and protecting appropriate limits on personal time and energy, and developing an expanded sense of personal identity beyond anti-violence work. One participant offers a clear example of setting limits in the name of personal well-being:

> My work does not have permission to intrude on my off time; my off time is my off time. When I'm on a day off, I don't check my messages. When I'm on a day off, I'm on a day off, and that's just the way it is, and I think part of it is because I understand what survivors these clients are!

Finally, it appears critical for anti-violence workers to balance an existential awareness of life and death with an appreciation for the greater context of life and growth:

> Things are so much about life and death that I do a lot of things like growing plants and things like that. I suppose a piece of it is always being able to preserve a sense of the sacred and beautiful because if you're doing this work and don't have that, I think it can get to you. If you don't have the ability to see the beautiful in things, I really don't think you're going to last doing this work.

Approach. A facilitative, empowering approach to helping is recommended by the participants as an important counterbalance to a helper's potential vulnerability to secondary traumatic stress. Such an approach emphasizes women's strengths and resources, supports them in making informed positive changes and respects their decisions as their own. Carefully guarding personal agendas within the helping relationship, incorporating a feminist analysis and emphasizing an element of hope appears to be further facilitative of helpers' well-being. For example, one participant poignantly expands on her beliefs about and approach to helping:

> [This work] is really about me helping [women] find their strength and their truth for their lives. If they need to stay, if they need to go, whatever it is ... I have nothing invested. I'm invested in their safety and in what they want. I tell you, it's been a hell of a lot easier for me to do this work since I've gotten to that point. But, early on, when I was frightened, when I thought I knew better [than the women], that was hell! I'm a facilitator [of change]. I'm not there to tell [women] what to do, I'm not there to judge them, and I'm not there to tell them that they have to get out. I am there to inform them so that they have the power of information. Often, as professionals, we expect to know it, to know it all, to lay it on! I think that domestic violence is just not like that. I am not a "therapist" with these women; I am a "witness," that's what I am.

A number of participants were clear about the need to have a feminist analysis of the relationship between power/control and violence/abuse in one's approach to anti-violence work. One participant was particularly clear about the importance of a feminist philosophy to her work:

> I think women take their relationships very seriously. Women go for counselling; they're in support groups; they go into 12 step programs; and they go to psychiatrists. [Women] are often told, "there's something wrong with you." So, the whole approach around "you're not crazy per se; the situation is [crazy], and that's left you feeling this way." You know, "your reactions are quite normal; they make sense to me given how you've been treated, how you've made sense of that, how you've coped with that."

Finally, several participants regard hope, especially when individual and social change is not so tangible, as a critical element in their approach to working with victims of violence and abuse. An attitude of hope also appears to foster personal enjoyment, job satisfaction and ongoing commitment to the anti-violence cause:

> My contribution might be a little piece of information, or it might just be to listen — that I had been there at that moment and that person felt listened to. All I ever have is the hope that maybe something that I did, even to give the person a bed for the night, made a difference in their life. But, there's nothing that you can do that is visible as a measure of "making a difference."

Workplace policy and practice. Although not a specific focus of this investigation, workplace policy and practice appears to be a prominent area that may serve to mitigate the symptoms and consequences of secondary traumatic stress. Administrative and collegial awareness of secondary traumatic stress, sensitive supervision, collegial support, open and respectful communication, promoting a degree of personal control within the employment context and ongoing organizational advocacy on behalf of anti-violence workers and abused women are important potential solutions to secondary traumatic stress. These are particularly important points of intervention, given the following participant's comment on the tendency, both within the anti-violence sector and beyond, to minimize and disregard anti-violence workers' vulnerability to secondary traumatic stress:

> There are a lot of people who do not believe we are affected by seeing this stuff over and over and over again. So, when someone does show signs of stress or trauma related to seeing all this stuff, sometimes they're judged like "well, what's the big deal? It's just an incident".

Another participant explicitly connects the costs associated with anti-violence work with professional, administrative and collegial awareness of secondary traumatic stress:

> I think there's a cost attached to this work that is not recognized by agencies. There needs to be more than just some money going for

> salary, whether that's extra time off or time for debriefing. [There's]
> also some built-in isolation in working in this field so that when
> you're just totally engrossed in a situation that takes you three days
> to work through with a person, you're not connecting with your
> colleagues because your colleagues are also so involved with what-
> ever; so, sometimes, I think, we unnecessarily carry around a lot of
> stuff that maybe 20 minutes of debriefing would rectify.

Several participants expanded on their vision of the importance of open,
supportive and constructively challenging communication in the workplace, particularly as it relates to secondary traumatic stress. For example:

> I would hope I never lose my compassion for a colleague who has
> these experiences. I would like to see us as a staff be able to talk
> about these things openly with each other and not feel like there's
> this expectation that, "oh, we're the helpers; we have to have it all
> together; this stuff doesn't affect us." Show [your colleagues] that,
> yes, it is a real thing when you do feel stressed out because a client
> shared something with you that was overly traumatic. It's okay to
> feel this way. It's okay to want to cry sometimes after you hear a
> [traumatic] story. You're human!

> The biggest thing that I think would be helpful would be the
> creation of an environment where people, where staff and policies
> and decisions could be challenged. Let's put them on the table —
> an environment where everybody is not so defensive, and has the
> attitude, "Let's look at this, and let's make changes according to
> the situation."

Several participants commented on the importance of professional
advocacy as it relates to reducing the potential costs of caring, particularly
in the name of cultivating a healthy workplace. For example, some workplace strategies may include striking committees specifically designed to
address the harmful effects of secondary traumatic stress. An ethic of team
work and enjoying positive relationships with relatively emotionally and
physically healthy colleagues with realistic performance expectations

appears imperative to countering the costs of caring:

> When you do the work that I do, I think it's really important to have a healthy environment, and for people to have realistic expectations, and to be able to support you — honestly support you and show that support.

Another participant expands on what she regards as an example of a positive workplace environment:

> There is a spoken and unspoken agreement that everybody who is here works towards making it a healthy place so that they are honouring and respectful of everyone — all the clients and each other. There is always someone to talk to, and staff are offered clinical counselling and supervision. We also have regular group meetings to discuss clinical cases and offer support and information to one another. It just feels very progressive and very respectful. Everybody here has the opportunity to be very independent. If you want to work one day a week, you can work one day a week. If you want to take three months off with no pay, you can do that too; it's very flexible.

Although not always possible within an organizational or agency context, some degree of influence over or input into workplace policy development, including policies related to caseload distribution and leave-from-work time, was appreciated, according to the comments of many participants. For example, one participant promotes the idea of restorative leave, which would enable front-line workers to monitor and take responsibility for when they need to retreat from anti-violence work as a preventative measure. Another participant enjoys a relative degree of control over her case/workload and elaborates on how she balances the intensity of her anti-violence work responsibilities:

> I can only book four [clients]. I'm always hoping for two "light" and two "heavy" [counselling sessions]. I will space [clients] so that I don't have four really heavy ones in one day. We have that

> power, and it makes you feel good that you have that control, and
> sometimes you make the wrong decision, but not always. You kind
> of get to know your women, and you know who really needs you
> right now, and who may be able to wait a bit.

It is important to note that crisis-oriented, short-term residential environments appear particularly difficult for front-line anti-violence counsellors.
These environments encourage a high degree of vigilance regarding personal and client safety and appear to pose particular challenges to personal
health. Furthermore, counsellor/client relationships within a shelter environment may often be of a short-term nature, leaving helpers to speculate
on the impact and outcome of their work in the absence of follow-up
contact with individual clients. One participant expands on her experience
within a short-term, emergency residential environment:

> [While working at the shelter] I found that I had colds a lot, and I
> had maybe head lice twice a year. The women were traumatized;
> they just weren't with it sometimes, and the counsellors had to
> take over which is really hard work.

However, another participant comments on the negative economic consequences associated with having some degree of control over her work life:

> I pick and choose my shifts for the most part, and that's how I
> achieve balance in my life — that's not going to bring me a strong
> pension; in fact, no pension at the end. That's kind of how I have
> balance, how I keep some distance, how I cope.

A number of participants commented on the connection between the
physical working environment and culture and feelings of marginalization
and compromised well-being as an anti-violence counsellor:

> An office with no windows and fluorescent lights, no heat control,
> a dingy little place, and being low down on the totem pole around
> what you can acquire, and having to go through 14 different chan-
> nels to get something like full-spectrum lighting installed is very

frustrating. [My] basic needs, so that I'm not distracted when working with people who are in crisis, and so that they're not uncomfortable. I'm stressed by driving through the inner city. I find that where we work is stressful in itself, you know, just in this area of the city? On my way home at night, I see so many incidents of deprivation and heartache and violence.

A couple of us are non-permanent staff members, so our jobs could be pretty much pulled at any point. There's always that sort of thing looming, that we're going to be doing that extra person's job and not having the benefit of an extra person to be connected with collegially.

Finally, in summarizing the importance of anti-violence workplace policy and practice and the power of one's personal career decision-making, one participant offers a cautionary comment:

Be careful where you work, and check it out for its professional affiliations and stewardship. Working in a place that has a Director who is healthy personally and wants to maintain a healthy workplace — where there are a lot of structures in place that allow that to happen. Get out of a place if it doesn't feel good, and go work elsewhere.

Systemic concerns. Many women commented on the fact that the women they seek to assist, along with their traumatic stories, are not the primary source of their discontent. Rather, systemic issues such as societal perspectives on violence and abuse, and the ongoing devaluation of women and women's work remain primary sources of strain for women working in the anti-violence field. From a solution-oriented perspective, these issues require ongoing, consistent advocacy within and on behalf of the anti-abuse field and abused women. Two participants poignantly expand on the systemic challenges associated with anti-violence work:

The challenges are sometimes our legal system around custody is unbelievable! I've got two cases right now where the men are extremely abusive, extremely abusive. One was even physically abusive to his children, but has shared custody! Both of the women are managing with good lawyers, but that means money, and a lot of our women do not have money. It's really stressful to find good representatives for them who really understand the cycle of violence. [Women] can remain in very abusive relationships when they're sharing custodial access. I have experienced, in recent years, a few really good judges that don't put up with this crap, but there are not enough of them out there. There are not enough lawyers that want to do this work who are good at it, and who understand the dynamics [of abusive relationships]!

A lot depends on who they get down in Social Services. Worker A might give them money for a bus pass to go to school; worker B might not. So much depends on the worker. Some judges are much more aware than others. I have become fairly skeptical, critical and cynical about Justice and Social Services. I don't think they understand the challenges women face when coming out of abusive situations.

In speaking to the lack of a feminist perspective, one participant comments on how larger ideological systems continue to support societal violence and abuse:

[Abuse] is still not recognized as a belief system, you know, an ideology ... Until [violence and abuse] is viewed in this way, it will be individual problems or individual solutions to problems.

We haven't grown very much and we don't place value on people — on women and children in particular. If [perpetrators] went into a store and stole $10,000.00, they'd be in jail just like that! But, they can beat up women or children, and be walking the streets in two days! So, where are our values?

Although all participants note that they are often more economically advantaged relative to their clientele, they also note that they can personally relate to their clients' experiences with poverty and marginalization:

> Women are kept poor and dependent — their options are very
> limited. You can almost relate [to the women] in a kind of way. I
> mean, I'm much better off than most of them, granted, but it is still
> that framework of [poverty]. I don't have a big glamorous house. I
> don't have fancy vehicles. I don't believe — maybe when my kids
> are older — but, I don't believe I could do this work full-time
> because of what it is, because of how it affects me, because of how
> hard it is. That's a decision I've made based on my own experience.
> I see, further down the road, some of the bigger complications and
> challenges. I have colleagues in their 50s who are quite poor, and
> one with no retirement savings.

Finally, the existing funding structures and the apparent lack of focus
on the importance of anti-violence work remains a profound stressor for
anti-violence workers. Many anti-violence workers struggle with a significant degree of employment insecurity, lack of appropriate remuneration,
overly demanding and crisis-oriented case/workloads, and short-staffing.
For example, one participant elaborates on this point:

> Funding is not secure; it is year-by-year. To me, this is torture! For
> an agency to function, I think the anti-violence movement, the
> domestic abuse movement, needs to get a little more real! I don't
> think we need to be cutting dollars; I think we need to be putting
> more dollars into the work.

Discussion

Implications for Professional Practice and Training
Results emerging from this investigation confirm that secondary traumatic
stress exists as a "clear and present danger" to anti-violence workers, as
well as an "occupational hazard" to the profession of front-line helping
(Richardson, 2001). As one participant aptly cautions:

> I do believe that there is a shelf life to front-line work. Front-line crisis counseling takes a toll. As solid as your boundaries, work ethic and supports may be, I think it does take a toll.

From a solution-oriented perspective, a number of participants offer clear recommendations for ameliorating secondary traumatic stress. These recommendations range from basic educational preparation and self-care health-oriented practices to promoting constructive work environments, cultivating nurturing personal and professional networks and maintaining a clear and realistic sense of identity as a helper.

This investigation confirms that secondary traumatic stress must be addressed by individuals, organizations, mental-health practitioners and relevant policy-makers as a very real occupational hazard for front-line anti-violence workers. Secondary traumatic stress appears to have an impact on work satisfaction, performance, and individual and organizational well being. Therefore, concerted educational initiatives are required to inform front-line anti-violence responders, students and organizations about the existence of and symptoms associated with secondary traumatic stress. From the perspective of prevention and early intervention, it is critical to destigmatize secondary trauma through organizational recognition and acknowledgment. Administrators and colleagues can have a positive impact on the well-being of front-line anti-violence responders by encouraging a climate of constructive communication, understanding and support in the workplace. For example, workplaces could move towards establishing policies that are consistent with the current state-of-knowledge of risk factors and prevention of secondary traumatic stress. In particular, this study shows that peer consultation, professional consultation, training and professional counselling represent some of the vital supports required by helpers. Finally, an empowerment, strength-based approach to the helping process is facilitative of helper well-being as it honours clients as resilient and capable and assists helpers in defining their appropriate roles relative to clients' healing journeys.

Future Research

For the purposes of an exploratory, depth-oriented study, the participant sample was necessarily small and self-selecting; therefore, quantitative data must be interpreted with caution, and are suggestive of the need for further and more complex investigation into front-line anti-violence counsellors' experiences of secondary traumatic stress and coping. The cross-sectional design also prevents causal inferences related to the development of secondary traumatic stress in vulnerable helpers. However, qualitative interviews yielded significant depth-oriented information and meaningful exemplars that would not have been derived from alternative methods.

Importantly, although comparative data is unavailable, the GSI suggests an increased rate of psychological distress in this particular participant sample at the time of investigation. Alternatively, the aggregate result for the CF sub-scale, which was designed as a measure of secondary traumatic stress in helping populations, suggests a non-concerning degree of this phenomenon in this sample, despite the numerous exemplars consistent with secondary traumatic stress. As a measure, the GSI may be tapping the cumulative and permanent impact of secondary traumatic stress left unchecked over time, whereas the CF taps more immediate symptoms resulting from acute incidents and exposure. Given these results, further investigations into this area should employ a multi-method, multi-measure approach.

Although scores on both CS and CF yielded average aggregate scores, the range of these scores indicates significant variability in individual experiences with front-line anti-violence work, secondary traumatic stress and coping. In fact, many participants commented on how their responses to anti-violence work changed on a temporal and historical basis. Some participants appeared positive in their reflections on secondary traumatic stress and coping, while others reported more challenges in this area. Given this variability, it may prove illuminating to examine the individual career and wellness trajectories of anti-violence workers to further elucidate the impact of intrapersonal, interpersonal, and environmental primary and secondary interventions on the experience and prevention of secondary traumatic stress.

In sum, moving towards a non-violent society means respecting that secondary traumatic stress is evident in the personal and professional lives of front-line anti-violence workers and that it has a bearing on the quality of the helping process. As researchers have determined, hurting care providers inhibit our efforts towards collective well-being and positive self- and community determination. Advocates, mental health care workers and organizations/agencies are all called upon to review how secondary traumatic stress is addressed within their respective contexts. We all benefit when the physical and emotional well-being of our care providers is regarded as an interventional and organizational policy priority.

CHAPTER NINE

The Power of Policy: *Anti-violence Workers Speak Their* Peace

Mary R. Hampton

T his chapter offers the perspective of anti-violence workers on existing policies designed to eliminate intimate partner violence (IPV). The "inclusive policy-making" model described by Wharf & McKenzie (1998) is the conceptual framework for this chapter; they suggest a participatory approach to policy-making that includes practitioners and service users to generate policy that truly meets the needs of recipient groups. Anti-violence workers are ideal participants for inclusive policy development; they have a unique vantage point for observing the effects of policy on their clients and are able to detect unforeseen consequences in implementation of some policies. Front-line anti-violence service providers are rarely included in policy development, yet these are the individuals who have direct experience with the reality of IPV. My premise is that they may know things about IPV that others don't.

Our focus on policy in this volume is consistent with governmental intent to strengthen public policy that is focused on eliminating intimate partner abuse. Policy profoundly affects victims of violence and those who work to eradicate violence in our society. Canadian responses to woman abuse have moved from treating violence as an individual aberration (prior to 1980) to its current focus on prevention; documents provided on gov-ern-mental websites suggest that woman abuse is accepted as a legitimate and important social issue (MacLeod & Kinnon, 1996). However, many feminist researchers have found a declining public awareness of the reality of IPV and no change in the dominant patriarchal ideologies that support violence against women (Gelles, 1997; Simon, Anderson, Thompson, Crosby, Shelley & Sacks, 2001). A common research finding is that policy-makers are often unaware that "unanticipated consequences of policies can create barriers for women who are abused and who try to seek help" (MacLeod & Kinnon, 1996, p. 34). An example of this is the active debate in the literature about recent increases in the number of women arrested for domestic violence. Is there truly a gender equivalency of violence, as some suggest, or is this an outcome of dual charging resulting from zero tolerance policies (Henning & Feder, 2004)? Anti-violence workers should be asked about these unanticipated consequences.

In this chapter, data are provided from eight qualitative interviews I conducted with anti-violence workers in the prairie provinces. The information they gave can inform us about the reality of anti-violence policy in the Canadian prairies. Eight women were asked how existing policies help or hinder them in their work. Policies are "framed by the ideologies and experiences of those who participate in the policy-making process" (Wharf & McKenzie, 1998, p. 122); therefore, it is essential to include the voices of those on the front lines so as to counter the dominant illusion that all is well and IPV is no longer a problem. These interviews offer a focused, but not comprehensive, critique of policies that are salient for these participants.

What do Anti-Violence Workers Think of Existing Policies?

Eight female anti-violence workers participated in this study. Six interviews were conducted face-to-face and two by telephone: Alberta (n=2), Saskatchewan (n=3), and Manitoba (n=3). Three of the participants work in northern areas of each province; the remaining five work in southern regions of the provinces. Four are shelter directors; two are front-line counsellors; one is a provincial coordinator of violence-prevention programs; and one develops anti-violence policy. Participants were recruited using purposive sampling procedures, drawing from a convenience sample of anti-violence workers, across the three prairie provinces, who are involved in a community/university research alliance funded by the Canadian government (Strauss & Corbin, 1998). As an academic partner in this research project, I had met many of these anti-violence workers previously. I sent an e-mail request to 18 community participants involved in this tri-provincial longitudinal research project, describing the purpose of this project and asking for an interview appointment at our tri-provincial meeting ("The Healing Journey," http://www.umanitoba.ca/resolve/). Eight of the community participants agreed to be interviewed. They have been working in this field an average of 15 years (range 4–26 years), so they have long-term commitments to the field of anti-violence work, and experience with shifting political climates that influence policy.

An open-ended interview format was used to explore their perspectives on the role of policies in any area related to their work (Rubin & Rubin, 1995). The workers were asked to reflect on all levels of policies, including local, provincial, and federal. They were prompted for the following systems: justice, child protection, shelter, and "others." They were specifically asked about the role of policy in the day-to-day work of anti-violence workers, how policies affect the lives of women abused by intimate partners, and were to identify policies that both help and hinder them in their work. Interviews were tape-recorded and transcribed for analysis. Grounded theory analytic procedures were used to generate a matrix (see Figure 1, p. 161) that describes both pluses and minuses of certain policies from the perspective of these participants (Strauss & Corbin, 1998). Feedback from the anti-violence workers is presented by theme. Anonymous quotations from participants illustrate each theme. Detailed analysis of provincial policies was not conducted, and perception of participants is the result of infor-mation that could be conveyed in one interview. Therefore, perspectives presented here offer only an initial attempt to convey anti-violence workers' experience with existing policies.

Justice Policies: Most Influential System

According to participants, policies in the justice system (criminal and family) exert the most influence on the lives of women who experience intimate partner violence. Interview participants had much to say about the impact of this system on their work. It appears that many policies have unintended consequences. Even the beneficial justice polices are often inconsistently administered. Four policies were described by all participants as helpful to women who experience intimate partner abuse.

1. *Zero Tolerance* policies of *mandatory charging* were cited as the most helpful: "I would say that the mandatory charging policy is a significant benefit." Participants stated that, overall, policies requiring police to charge a suspected perpetrator of violence protect the women and help anti-violence workers in their jobs. One shelter director stated:

   > I like the policy of the police laying charges when they see evidence of an assault. The onus is no longer entirely on the victim to testify ... that general policy is a good one and a sound one. I think it's been shown that more than anything else it reduces repeat offences of domestic violence.

2. Policies that require *notifying victims* when a violent offender is about to be released from incarceration are helpful, but inconsistently administered. A front-line counsellor said: "I like the policy of notifying the victims when a violent offender is about to be released. The policy is really good, but we don't always see this happening in actuality."

3. Policies offering *restitution programs* for victims are present in one province and are helpful to workers and victims.

4. *Emergency Protection Orders* (EPOs) were also described as helpful. Police will escort women home to retrieve their belongings after they enter shelters. However, many women are not aware that there is a time limitation for escort (24 hrs.), after which she needs a court order to retrieve "even a toothbrush."

Participants described five issues that appear to be unintended consequences of justice policies or issues that need policy adjustment.

1. The new phenomenon of *dual charging* is a consequence of mandatory charging policy, and was cited by participants across all three provinces as the most problematic aspect of the justice system. Zero Tolerance policy has been interpreted by many provincial Attorneys General as "gender-neutral": that is, women who call for police

intervention in a violent incident may also be charged with assault. Even if she has been defending herself *against* violence. Participants stated that charges against male perpetrators are sometimes not laid if women fight back. One shelter director gave an example of this:

> The woman came into the shelter very beat. And in the course of the violence she got a few shots in at him. She was hospitalized and then came out of the hospital, but he had to have medical attention, too, for a scratch and things like that. And I'm not downplaying but they wouldn't charge him because he had injuries, too. So the fact that she kind of hit back a little bit negated the fact that severe abuse happened.

One participant constructs provincial anti-violence policy, and observed that double or dual charging "creates a perceived barrier for victims who reach out for help, unwarranted backlogs in the court system, increased stay rates of charges, service barriers (women can't get help from some services if there are outstanding domestic violence charges against them), and unanticipated involvement with child protection agencies."

To remedy this unanticipated consequence, some urban centres are considering policy changes directed at the "primary aggressor." Several participants stated that these changes have been helpful in the U.S., and suggest that we implement this strategy in Canada: "some training around primary aggressor [has resulted] in their dual charging going down significantly within a period of years."

2. *Mandatory charging* was described as a policy that protects women who experience intimate partner violence, but also as problematic. Many abused women no longer call the police for help because they know their partner must be charged with assault. All participants believe that mandatory charging is essential, but several agreed with one shelter director that, "what has happened here is that women no longer call the police. They don't want to call the police; they don't want the police involved because they know the police will charge." Research that relies on numbers of arrests to document cases of intimate partner abuse must consider the impact of this unforeseen consequence when counting cases. Statistics that suggest

prevalence of IPV is decreasing may be influenced by the reality that abused women may not be calling the police when they need to.

Participants also stated that mandatory charging is not always implemented by police officers, even though the intent of this policy is to eliminate police discretion (Ursel, 2002). Specialized units, such as domestic crimes units, were described as excellent, but generally police officers lack adequate training in IPV response. A common experience expressed by participants is: "I would say that the mandatory charging policy is a significant benefit.... If it's a [police officer] on the street, we still don't get mandatory charging, but if it's [specialized unit], they do a really good job overall."

Participants stated that, as part of their anti-violence work, they foster collaboration between themselves and front-line justice workers. A shelter director who works in the northern region of a province described this active networking: "We've developed a good working relationship with the RCMP in our area where they refer a lot of clients to us and they assist us if we have a situation."

These positive relationships are a result of education provided by anti-violence workers:

> We've got plans to meet together and educate the employees on some of the domestic violence issues. Because they're a bunch of young guys and women there that need to know you don't give out the address of shelters to men that are looking for the women.

Another participant said, "I lecture to the recruits of the Police College." All agree that "there's a lot of work to do within the shelter movement, not just dealing with the violence but it's the educational part, too."

3. Another issue that could be addressed through policy adjustment is *long waits for court dates*: "It's very frustrating for women when these things are going to court and it takes months and months and months. So if her husband's charged with assault, he may not show up in court for close to a year."

Participants stated that, unless there is a specialized legal unit such as the family court, there is a general lack of understanding about intimate partner violence in the justice system. Winnipeg's family court system was cited by many participants as a model for other provinces.

4. *Custody and access* policies were described as extremely problematic for women. In Saskatchewan and Alberta, there is no communication between the family and criminal courts in most jurisdictions; women are often caught between these two separate systems. Joint custody and unsupervised visits by the offender are often responsible for putting children at risk, for continued abuse of the victim, and even homicide. One program director has observed this problem many times:

> The custody issues are huge. There's no connection in communication between the different courts. The numbers of women and children every year who are caught in the middle between criminal court and family court are huge. If the person who is abusive towards them has their act together in a negative kind of way, they'll get to family court before the woman does and so the women and children are in shelter and the abuser will have gone to family court and got an order to access, unsupervised access often, or custody, in the time frame that custody is being determined. And so it's very, very difficult, and just horror stories around that. The judgments that are very often rendered put women and children at serious risk and there are a number of examples of that. Two specific examples of that that I can think of over the last two and a half years in our province where there has been unsupervised access granted and little ones are dead and their moms are dead.

5. *Emergency Protection Orders* (EPOs) were described as helpful, but also bureaucratically cumbersome. One shelter director stated: "Emergency Protection Orders were legislated a few years ago and there's been variable implementation of that throughout the province and it hasn't been utilized very well or often. The police associated with it have not interpreted it or been trained well." For example, police officers can make an arrest for violation of an EPO, as well as

retrieve a child from a non-custodial parent, yet additional rein-forcement court orders are needed for these interventions. A shelter director from a rural area described this situation:

> There's the new legislation which allows for Emergency Protection Orders in our province which keeps him away from his home without a court hearing for a short period of time until it can be heard in court. There was an instance where a woman had one of those, she was repeatedly stalked and harassed by her ex-partner; the police made an arrest for violation of an EPO and the police officer was scolded by the judge for making the arrest without going to the crown prosecutor and getting permission to enforce the order. Then the judge softened the conditions of the EPO, in effect rewarding the offender for violating the EPO.

Participants stated that women who leave abusive relationships often do not have access to legal aid to help them negotiate the justice system.

Child Protection Policies: Good Idea, But Does It Work?
During the interviews, child protection policies generated heated responses from participants. They find that child protection policies both help and hinder them in their work. Only one policy was cited by participants as uniformly helpful to women abused by intimate partners:

Home/Respite Care can be accessed in one province by families caught in the cycle of violence:

> Home care and respite as a means of intervention and support for families caught in the cycle of violence are welcomed by the family for a myriad of reasons. The assistance of another pair of hands is no doubt appreciated. More importantly, though, the perception that child welfare agencies can become involved with a struggling family and not apprehend the children in that family goes even further in encouraging the family to stay the course of intervention and service access.

Overall, anti-violence workers support legislation of child protection policies, but are frustrated with the implementation of these policies and the
unanticipated effect on abused women.

Three policies were discussed at length by participants; these policies
generated ambivalent responses.

1. *Mandatory reporting of child abuse* is considered a policy that both
    helps and hinders anti-violence work, particularly in a shelter con-
    text. One anti-violence worker described the situation her clients
    face: "I come into the shelter as a client; it's supposed to be a refuge;
    it's supposed to be a safe haven; and the kids get taken away. Now
    what kind of shelter is this?" Child protection workers have been
    known to house clients in shelters, saying to them, "If you don't go
    to the shelter, you lose your kids." Moms may come into the shelter
    under this threat, even though these women are not perpetrating
    violence on the children. Participants agree that children need to be
    protected, so they support legislation such as *Child Welfare Acts*;
    however, interpretation and implementation of these policies can
    negatively affect their clients.

    Participants said that they can interpret policies in ways that
    help rather than hinder their work. For example, in Manitoba, the
    Child and Family Services Act, Part 3, identifies the "domestic envi-
    ronment" as a measurable element in the assessment of need for
    intervention. Anti-violence workers find that this wording is flexible
    enough to allow for interpretation; therefore, workers can invoke
    this section of the *Act*, relying on the open language, to advocate for
    clients when child protection is not warranted. This allows for more
    flexible interpretation of mandatory reporting, because circum-
    stances vary widely from one case to another. On the other hand,
    mandatory reporting of child abuse relieves the service providers
    from responsibility for determining the "strength of a case." The
    best case scenario occurs when child apprehension is not a reaction-
    ary solution to every reported problem, but can be perceived as an
    opportunity for a family to become connected to the most relevant
    supports at a time of need.

Another significant problem is that child welfare agencies may seek permanent wardship of children while mothers are actively engaged in ending the abuse in their lives. A program coordinator stated:

> When child welfare agencies seek permanent wardship of children whose mothers are in such residential care programs while those mothers are receiving support, they undermine those mothers' efforts to get well and to reconnect with her children. For many women, then, reaching out for help is not an option if losing their children is a possibility.

Women who have witnessed these cases often do not reach out for help if losing their children is a possibility.

2. *Child Protection Acts* that mandate legal protection for children who witness violence can be problematic for anti-violence workers and for women who suffer intimate partner violence. Participants stated that this policy affects at least half of their clients who return to abusive situations, and they feel that, unless women are clearly informed about the limits of confidentiality, the policy can undermine the trust they hope to establish with women:

> That impacts our work quite drastically because, for instance, if half of your women go back home, that's a bit of a high percentage, but a significant number do. So if they decide to go back home and if they have children, which is also a high proportion of the women who come in, and if they have experienced violence, which is everyone that comes in, those children all have to be protected. So that is half of our clients right there. So a major impact.

Shelter workers have developed consent forms that include these policies, making it very clear that they are mandated to report situations where they know children have witnessed abuse. They have had to become clearer in the wording of their consent forms so that women understand the limits of confidentiality and the potential for apprehension of their children. A shelter director stated: "Before they start telling their life story, they know what the rules are; they know what we will do with the information; they understand when they sign this confidentiality form that information about harm to their children will be released to the department."

Participants believe that, from a worker's standpoint, this is generally a good policy. They stated that it is important to recognize "the damage done to children when they witness abuse." However, participants expressed their ambivalence about this policy by saying:

> It helps us protect children, which is part of our job, [but] it has made communal living in the shelter situation more difficult. Because you've got women coming in that are beaten and they're traumatized. The children, in most cases, have heard or seen this and they're very needy for their mom.

Taking these children away from moms at this point further traumatizes both parties.

Anti-violence workers state that child welfare units have huge caseloads and usually do not have specialized units dealing with domestic violence. Participants stated that child protection workers will investigate cases where children have witnessed abuse, and typically will require that the mother leave the abusive relationship or lose her children. If the mother leaves the relationship, there are inadequate supports for her to maintain independence and negotiate custody through the court systems. One shelter director stated:

> With all the cuts that have been made to social programs in the last decade or so, there's reduced eligibility for Legal Aid. And most of the Legal Aid money now goes to people charged with criminal offences, to defend themselves in court, and a woman cannot even get Legal Aid in a custody battle unless her partner also has a lawyer. So if he's defending himself in court, she can't get a lawyer through Legal Aid.

The child welfare system will often refer her to another system (custody and access = family court), rather than offer her support to make the changes they require. An example of creative problem-solving was initiated by Alberta's Council of Women's Shelters. This group conducts joint training for child welfare and shelter workers and has developed collaborative working relationships between systems to ameliorate potential damage to abused women who "fall between the cracks." There is a policy in that province offering financial support to mothers when they've left an abusive relationship, as an alternative to removing children. Anti-violence workers know that emotional harm is done to children when they are exposed to domestic violence in the home; however, they believe that policies that punish the mother [the victim] are unfair.

3. Another problematic policy within child welfare agencies requires workers to contact non-custodial parents; in IPV cases this can result in workers letting perpetrators know the location of the victim. He (the perpetrator) may not have previously known where the child or the mother was living; this can create additional safety risks for a woman and her children by focusing, in the most narrow way, on the possible well-being of the child.

Shelter Policies: Consistent and Helpful

Policies within shelters across the provinces were described as consistent. The biggest shelter problem is inadequate funding for victim services. Participants agree with the policies of security, confidentiality, and support that help them keep women safe. Although not a shelter policy, anti-violence workers described a lack of awareness among the general public about the severity of IPV, which requires them to constantly prove the need for their existence. Similar to Martin's (this volume) findings, the need for safe shelter is obvious to our participants, but may not be acknowledged by the general public: "A lot of people just don't think that it's a big problem anymore. They've taken care of it." The experience of participants in this study suggests that the prevalence of IPV is not decreasing; there is a growing need for more resources. For example, a northern Saskatchewan community built a new shelter, expanded its resources, and "provided 1,128 more bedments last year; and by bedments that means we have a woman or a child in a bed; so it's well over 5,500 more last year. So there's a need, definitely a need." This need is most urgent in rural and remote locations.

Participants mentioned two policies that hinder their work; both are a result of inadequate funding.

1. One shelter policy that is problematic for anti-violence workers is limited stays, which is a response to inadequate funding. As one participant stated, "You don't change a woman's life in ten days. You do give her a few tools; you can help her facilitate some processes.... It would be nice sometimes to have a longer relationship." Provinces have different policies limiting women's stay in shelters, with Alberta's being the shortest: "It just isn't realistic, and the woman is not able to make arrangements for herself and her family in time." Participants stated that funding for follow-up would help this situation.

2. Shelters, in most areas, do not receive funding to do follow-up and education. According to one participant:

> We have to fundraise for things like follow-up visits after women set up their own households, and public education on domestic violence, even though we regard these as essential services that we must do no matter where we find the money to do them.

Present policies describe this as duplication of services that exist in other agencies. However, participants stated that women can "get lost, because with the women only being there an average of ten days, you still build up a relationship and trust, and then when you send them off and you refer them to another worker, they've got to rebuild that again." Many shelters do their own fundraising to support follow-up, or even do this work above and beyond their already heavy workload. Manitoba recently provided funding for a position in shelters to do this follow-up work. However, in the other two provinces participants were confused about whether the policy against funding follow-up was a provincial or federal policy, or merely an "unwritten policy." In most provinces, provincial funding also does not cover second-stage housing. Participants have heard it said, "We will never fund second-stage housing; you are welcome to set up second-stage housing, but we will not fund it." They do not know, however, whether this is a "written policy."

Mental Health/Social Service Policies: Could Be Doing More

Two additional systems have a profound impact on the lives of women who experience intimate partner abuse. Mental health and social service policies are potential sources of support that anti-violence workers describe as generally inadequate. In the social service system, two policies are seen as helpful.

1. The database and standardized exit interview used in Alberta facilitates statistics and tracking of women.
2. A policy in Alberta stating that women who leave abusive relationships are given a sum of money. As with other policies, however, bureaucratic difficulties often interfere with disbursement of these funds, so this policy is unevenly implemented. One worker reflects: "So generally our supports for independence do not support women leaving ... even that $1,000, I mean, that's peanuts. You can't live on what that policy gives."

Unhelpful social service policies are those that are bureaucratically cumbersome.

1. In Saskatchewan, centralization of the social-assistance register has caused many difficulties for women and for shelter workers. Women need to telephone and make an appointment, which can mean they will be on the phone for up to an hour waiting for assistance, tying up essential phone services and requiring increased child-care support.
2. Bureaucratic requirements for abused women waiting to access social assistance can also put them in danger by requiring that they physically leave the shelter and jump through many hoops before they are helped.
3. Lack of policies providing for affordable housing was cited by participants in all three provinces as a significant barrier for women leaving abusive relationships. One shelter director stated: "the whole political environment in the last decade of government retrenchment on social programs has been very detrimental to abused women; it's really affected their ability to maintain their economic independence after they leave an abusive relationship." Social assistance does not provide adequate financial assistance to help women with this. A program director stated that:

47 percent of women between January and June of 2003 returned to their partners when they left emergency shelters because of lack of resources, either affordable housing, or financial. Now that information, which we never had before concretely, caused a change in policy in our supports for independence, which suggests that every woman leaving an abusive relation-ship in Alberta gets $1,000 and it doesn't matter if she leaves once or ten times. Every time she's supposed to get $1,000 without any questions asked. Now in practice does that happen? No.

Health and mental health policies present difficulties for anti-violence workers. Some women who enter shelters also have mental health or addiction problems. There are limited numbers of psychiatric beds available for chronically ill individuals, and inadequate treatment facilities, so women with addiction and/or mental health problems may end up in a shelter for abused women due to multiple issues. A shelter director in an urban area stated:

> But what's frustrating with women with both substance problems and mental health problems is you want to move them on, but there's no place for them to go. You have to be the bad guy and not only that but what you're doing is you're removing one person because of the safety generally for everybody.... if she goes, there's no place for her to go; there's no help but you have to say, "I can't care. I have to care about the 15 that are here ... to protect them."

It is also difficult to get psychiatric consultations in shelters as well as emergency treatment in hospital:

> If we take a woman in who has mental health issues, and we do that all the time, and if they are not well and can't live communally, it disrupts the whole entire house; then we have other people leaving because they can't live with the disruption. And we try to get help for the woman who is ill.

> I've taken women to Emergency and waited for a psychiatrist,
> who says she's fine, they won't take her in, or there's no bed.

In rural and remote areas, shelters are described as "multi-use," meaning "we take other women in crisis and transient women in the community." However, lack of policies providing comprehensive community programming, that supports people with serious mental illness, affects operations of these shelters.

Discussion

I refer back to the premise presented in the beginning of this chapter: anti-violence workers may know things that others don't and, therefore, are essential contributors to effective policies designed to eliminate intimate partner violence. Analysis of interviews with these eight anti-violence workers suggests that this is indeed the case. Anti-violence workers know that violence against women is a fundamental ideology of the patriarchal system we live in, so much an engrained part of the fabric of our society that it is invisible to policy-makers. As one interview participant stated, "Violence against women is in epidemic proportions in our country."

They know from direct experience that it can be more difficult for women to leave abusive relationships than to stay in them, contrary to popular opinion. As two shelter directors (M and C) stated:

> M: When women come to the shelter you plant the seed, okay? And you tend to that seed while they're in the shelter. But then they leave. Well, that seed's not going to germinate and grow unless there's someone there to help. You need lots of things for a crop to grow. Well, you need lots of things for women to lead a violence-free life. And you know, they're getting the seed, and they're getting a little bit of fertilizer and rainwater there, but when they leave it's a drought.

> C: And people still sometimes don't give full credit to how difficult it is to make that change. It's more difficult to leave a dysfunctional relationship than it is to leave a functional one. Because if he's so nasty, it must be easier to leave. Well, that's not necessarily true.

According to participants, the two factors that are most important in supporting women leaving abusive relationships are: (1) legal support; and (2) economic self-sufficiency. This finding is similar to Gelles' (1976) conclusions. Unintended consequences of existing policies and fragmented services can undermine achievement of these two factors. The problem of intimate partner violence cuts across many systems; because of this, women who need help can fall through the cracks or find it impossible to negotiate the complexities of differing systems.

Interrelationships

Much of what the participants share is discussed in the literature, but these participants see interrelationships where others don't. Gill's chapter (this volume) discusses various theoretical explanations for intimate partner violence, only one of which focuses on systems and contexts. Even research focusing on systems that maintain violence in our society often does not see the interrelationships between systems as clearly as these participants do. Reflecting on anti-violence workers' experience with policy, I observed that the policies of multiple systems affect lives of women abused by intimate partners. In Figure 1 on the next page, I suggest a simple diagram: women who experience abuse are placed at the centre of concentric systems that do not regularly relate to each other.

Anti-violence workers are depicted as "holding," or providing a context of safety for women who have been abused. Policies that were mentioned by participants in this study are listed within each system and critiqued as either helpful (+) or negative (−) in their impact on abused women. Many policies are considered helpful, yet participants also identified unforeseen negative consequences for their clients. Some policies have both positive and negative (+/−) effects on the lives of women abused by intimate partners.

Policies of the justice system have the largest impact on the lives of women who have experienced intimate partner violence. Mandatory charging and zero tolerance were cited by all participants as essential for helping anti-violence workers do their job. However, as Ursel (2002) points out, the traditional criminal justice approach does not adequately address the complex nature of domestic violence. Participants noted that mandatory-charging policies are essential for women's safety, but may have unintended

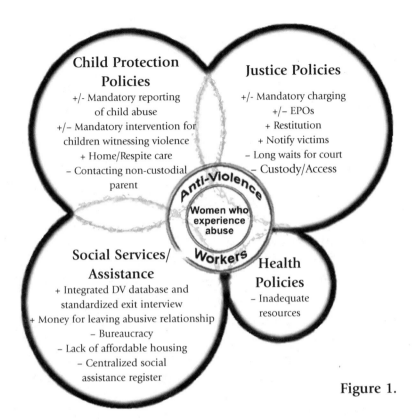

Figure 1.

negative consequences because women may not call police for help when it is sorely needed.

All participants stated that specialized services such as family-violence courts, specialized correctional programs, and domestic violence coordinators within police services are needed to adequately implement these policies. Integrated, specialized systems that specifically address the unique aspects of IPV are more likely to be helpful to women. For example, there is evidence that women in Manitoba who have access to the Family Violence Court are more likely than women in other provinces to call for police intervention (Statistics Canada, 1999/2000; Ursel, 2002).

Ursel's research (2002) suggests that public opinion supports mandatory charging and zero tolerance, yet these policies also come under attack in public media. Empirical research has demonstrated a link between public awareness and criminal justice policies:

The enactment of criminal justice policies, therefore, may have an impact beyond victims and perpetrators and lead to a transformation of the community through the emergence of new social norms. Public awareness campaigns designed to disseminate criminal justice policies may be instrumental in provoking social change (Salazar, Baker, Price, & Carlin, 2003).

All participants in this study expressed frustration with high public tolerance of intimate partner violence; public awareness combined with consistently enforced criminal justice policies are recommended.

Helpful policies, such as zero tolerance, have inadvertently led to the problematic dual charging phenomenon. Empirical research conducted with females and males arrested for domestic assault supports our participants' observations that there is not an "equivalency of violence" between genders and that women continue to be unfairly disadvantaged by the dual charging phenomenon (Henning & Feder, 2004). Another problem pointed out by our participants is that the bureaucracy involved in the criminal justice system leaves women in vulnerable positions since many women who use police services to stop violence have inadequate economic resources and need to rely on diminishing social services such as Legal Aid (Ursel, 2002). Some helpful policies have been implemented as a result of the *Victims of Domestic Violence Act,* such as Emergency Protection Orders that mandate access to home and belongings following a violent incident (Rodgers, 1994). However, participants stated that 24 hours is not sufficient time to allow for this access. I also heard, as did Tutty and Goard (2002), that women are often not safe, even when escorted. For example, anti-violence workers have found the male abuser hiding in the house when they accompanied women home to collect belongings.

Child protection policies that require mandatory reporting when children witness violence are a concern to participants. Canadian provinces are now including specific clauses in their child protection legislation that cite exposure to violence within the home as a form of child abuse. Anti-violence workers in our sample are ambivalent about this policy. Over 75 percent of women who come to transition houses have children (Statistics Canada, 1999/2000). Despite a decline in the number of children admitted to shelters, the proportion of children in shelters for reasons of child abuse increased from 1998 to 2000 — 86 percent of children residing in shelters in 1998 were there for reasons of child abuse compared to 91 percent of children in 2000 (Statistics Canada, 2001). Most of these children were under the age of five. Nixon (2002) states that one of the problems with mandatory reporting legislation is that the language is "gender-neutral," using terms such as "domestic violence" or "domestic disharmony," which does not acknowledge the fact that victims are almost always women and children. Therefore, child protection policies further victimize abused women and tend to ignore abusive men (Nixon, 2002). The child welfare system focuses on the responsibility of mothers to protect their children, ignoring the responsibility of the male abuser. The phenomenon of "mother-blaming" is a fundamental aspect of patriarchal ideology; so this policy reinforces "the dramatic contrast between our culture's readiness to *blame* mothers for any problems in their children and its tendency to *excuse* men when they commit hurtful or violent acts" (Caplan & Caplan 1999, p. 75). Supports are not provided to women who are victims; instead, women are seen as negligent and inadequate parents. An unanticipated consequence of some child welfare policies has had the opposite effect from the one intended, with women staying in abusive situations rather than risk losing their children. Nixon (2002) suggests that policies should clearly state that responsibility for the abuse lies in the perpetrator, and should prevent future contact between this parent and the children, not between the victim [mother] and children. Internationally, it is recognized that custody and access to children after divorce must be evaluated differently when it is known that domestic violence has occurred (Pope, Butcher & Seelen, 1994).

The social assistance system also influences abused women. Many women who use shelters are among the most vulnerable, with few economic resources (Dobash, Dobash, Cavanagh & Lewis, 2000). Women abused by intimate partners are strongly affected by the political environment; for instance, retrenchment on social programs and reduction of welfare rates have been very detrimental to abused women, affecting their ability to maintain economic independence. Participants cite lack of resources as a major reason women return to abusive situations. Shelters in some provinces don't receive funding for support services that they could be offering. Participants did not know whether there actually is a "written policy" against certain duplication of services. They stated that follow-up assistance they could be providing clients does not in reality overlap with other services.

The Canadian government has suggested that effects of violence pose major health risks: physical trauma, long-term disability, depression, alcohol/drug dependence, suicidal behaviours, low birth-weight babies, etc. (MacLeod & Kinnon, 1996). However, our participants state that the health care system provides inadequate supports for women abused by intimate partners. Resources such as treatment programs are often targeted at male abusers. Treatment programs for batterers rightly fall under the justice system; in fact, the most common sentence imposed on batterers is probation and court-mandated treatment, yet a minimum of two years' treatment has been found to be needed in most situations to change male batterer's behaviours and this amount of time is not usually given (Dutton & Golant, 1995; Hamberger & Ambuel, 1997; Ursel, 2002). Health and mental health supports for victims who suffer abuse and are often further abused by the system are inadequate. As one participant stated: "That's very unfortunate and very unfair because it seems that, again, all the services and privileges are geared to the offender and protecting the offender from false charges or undue punishment and not aimed at protecting the victim."

Prevalence of post-traumatic stress disorder and other physical and mental health effects of abuse are well-documented (Astin, Lawrence & Foy, 1993; Tutty & Rothery, 2002). We would caution against providing a psychiatric diagnosis for women abused by intimate partners; however, acknowledging the health impact of living in daily fear warrants care from our health system. Shelters are often used as a "last resort" or refuge for women with mental health and addiction problems. Participants stated that women who are abused and also have these mental health problems are appropriate for shelter. However, due to lack of health and mental health infrastructure, some women suffering primarily from psychiatric problems are inappropriately housed in shelters. This is particularly true in rural areas. Previous research has demonstrated that shelters and support groups are essential for the mental health of women abused by intimate partners (Molden, 2002; Tutty & Rothery, 2002). Walker (1999) states that support groups provided by shelters are often sufficient for supporting women in their healing. However, these authors also conclude that emergency shelter with limited stay is inadequate to support transition to a violent-free life. Provision of ongoing counselling and support for women specific to post-traumatic stress has been proven to be helpful and should be provided.

Vision of a Violence-Free World

The figure presented in this chapter is limited in its critique of policies, but can be adapted to reflect your experience. For example, two encompassing circles should be added to the figure: (1) the political environment which has an impact on policy development and implementation; and (2) existing patriarchal ideologies, which would be the largest circle encompassing all other material. DeKeseredy & Ellis (1995) conclude that, while many of the current policies may be helpful in the short run, they will not eliminate the deeper roots of intimate partner violence that are grounded in structural economic inequalities and patriarchal ideologies.

Challenges to the patriarchal ideology that allows for continuation of violence against women has come from women like our participants. As Ursel (1992) states, aggressive lobbying by women across Canada has challenged the patriarchal social tolerance of wife abuse and demonstrated that it is costly, both in monetary and social capital. Despite their exclusion from public policy discourse, I found that anti-violence workers are purposely creating collaborative networks with police, RCMP, child-custody workers, and social service agencies. Integrated services were described by all participants as essential for seamless, safe care for abused women and children.

A larger vision of a violence-free society sustains our participants in their long-term commitment to this cause. Language used to describe their work is important; participants prefer use of the term "anti-violence" to diminished terms such as "shelter" worker because, "if the work we do is anti-violence focused as opposed to ongoing support, which is available in the community, perhaps we have to give ourselves more credit and be specific in what service it is that we offer." Research on IPV should also include discourse analysis of policy language such as the use of "gender-neutral" language to describe a gender-specific phenomenon such as woman abuse.

Anti-violence workers state that their goal is to support "women in a violence-free lifestyle." This goal is important, because "the individual cases are just so awful, so awful." Ultimately, all participants are sustained by a vision that "the end of the cycle is that our systems will support equity, and all the 'isms,' including gender, will be evaporated, and we'll live in a community in a way that we'd like to be and that would be violence-free." As I listened to reflections of the participants in this study, I was struck by the importance of comprehensive, province-specific analysis of policy implementation that includes multiple data sources: quantitative data such as police data, public opinion, and, especially, the perspectives of service providers and clients.

References

Alksnis, C. (2001). Fundamental justice is the issue: Extending full equality of the law to women and children. *Journal of Social Distress and the Homeless,* *10,* 69–86.

American Psychiatric Association (2000). *Diagnostic and statistical manual of mental disorders* (4th ed.). Washington, D.C.: The American Psychiatric Association.

Amnesty International (2004). *Stolen Sisters: A human rights response to discrimination and violence against Indigenous women in Canada.* [on-line at: http://www.amnesty.ca/resource_centre/reports/view.php] Application of s. 718.2(e) of the Criminal Code: *R. v. Gladue* in *Justice as Healing, 4,* (Summer 1999).

Arvay, M.J. (2001). Secondary traumatic stress and trauma counsellors: What does the research say? *International Journal for the Advancement of Counselling, 23,* 283–293.

Astin, M., Lawrence, K. & Foy, D. (1993). Posttraumatic stress disorder among battered women: Risk and resiliency factors. *Violence and Victims, 8,* 17–28.

Ateah, C.A. & Mirwaldt, J. (Eds.) (2004). *Within our reach: Preventing abuse across the lifespan.* Nova Scotia & Manitoba: Fernwood Publishing & RESOLVE.

Austin, J.B. & Juergen, D. (1999). Standards for batterer programs: A review and analysis. *Journal of Interpersonal Violence, 14,* 152–167.

Backhouse, C. (1991). *Petticoats and prejudice: Women and law in nineteenth century Canada.* Toronto: Women's Press.

Bandura, A. (1971). *Social learning theory.* Morristown, NJ: General Learning.

Bannerji, H. (1993). Popular images of south Asian women. In H. Bannerji (Ed.), *Returning the gaze: Essays on racism, feminism and politics* (pp. 144–152). Toronto: Sister Vision.

Baranowsky, A.B. (2002). The silencing response in clinical practice: On the road to dialogue. In C.F. Figley (Ed.), *Treating compassion fatigue: Psychosocial stress series* (pp. 155–170). New York: Brunner-Routledge.

Barnett, O.W., Miller-Perrin, C.L. & Perrin, R.D. (1997). *Family violence across the lifespan.* Newbury Park, CA: Sage Publications.

Bean, C.A. (1992). *Women murdered by the men they loved.* New York: The Haworth Press.

Belknap, J. (1995). Law enforcement officers' attitudes about the appropriate responses to woman battering. *International Review of Victimology, 4,* 47–62.

Bergen, R.K. (1998). The reality of wife rape: Women's experiences of sexual violence in marriage. In R.K. Bergen (Ed.), *Issues in intimate violence* (pp. 237–250). Thousand Oaks, CA: Sage Publications.

Berger, H. (2001). Trauma and the therapist. In T. Spiers (Ed.), *Trauma: A practitioner's guide to counseling* (pp. 189–212). New York: Brunner-Routledge.

Black, D. & Reiss, A.J. Jr. (1967). Patterns of behavior in police and citizen transactions. In *Studies of crime and law enforcement in major metropolitan areas.* President's Commission on Law Enforcement and the Administration of Justice, Field Surveys III, Vol. 2. Washington, D.C.: U.S. Government Printing Office.

Bonnycastle, K. & Rigakos, G. (1998). *Unsettling truths: Battered women policy, politics, and contemporary research in Canada.* Vancouver: Collective Press.

Bowker, L. (1993). A battered woman's problems are social not psychological. In R.J. Gelles & D.R. Loseske (Eds.), *Current controversies on family violence* (pp. 154–165). Newbury Park, CA: Sage Publications.

Brown, J. (1997). Working toward freedom from violence: The process of change in battered women. *Violence Against Women: An International and Interdisciplinary Journal, 3,* 5–6.

Browne, A. (1993). Violence against women by male partners. *American Psychologist, 48,* 1077–1087.

Brzozowski, J.A. (Ed.) (2004). *Family violence in Canada: A statistical profile 2004.* Statistics Canada: Canadian Centre for Justice Statistics.

Buel, S.M. (1988). Mandatory arrest for domestic violence. *Harvard Women's Law Journal, 11,* 213–226.

Burstow, B. (1992). *Radical feminist therapy: Working in the context of violence.* Newbury Park, CA: Sage Publications.

Buzawa, E.S. & Buzawa, C.G. (2002). *Domestic violence. The criminal justice response* (3rd ed.). Thousand Oaks, CA: Sage Publications.

Campbell, J.C. (1986). Nursing assessment for risk of homicide with battered women. *Advances in Nursing Science, 8,* 36–51.

Campbell. J.C. (1992). If I can't have you, no one can. In J. Radford & D. Russell (Eds.), *Femicide: The politics of woman killing* (pp. 99–108). New York: Twayne.

Campbell, J.C. (1998). Abuse during pregnancy: Progress, policy and potential. *American Journal of Public Health, 88,* 185-187.

Campbell, J.C., Sharps, P.W. & Glass, N. (2000). Risk assessment for intimate partner violence. In G. Pinard & L. Pagani (Eds.), *Clinical assessment of dangerousness: Empirical contributions* (pp. 136–157). New York: Cambridge University Press.

Campbell, J.C., Webster, D., Koziol-McLain, J., Block, C., Campbell, D., Curry, M., Gary, F., Glass, N., McFarlane, J., Sachs, C., Sharps, P., Ulrich, Y., Wilt, S., Manganello, J., Xu, X., Schollenberger, J., Frye, V. & Laughon, K. (2003). Risk factors for femicide in abusive relationships: Results from a multi-site case control study. *American Journal of Public Health, 93,* 1089–1097.

Campbell, M.E. (1999). Case Comment: *R. v. Gladue.* 4 *Can. Crim. L.R.,* 237–241.

Canadian Centre for Justice Statistics (2000). Family violence in Canada: A statistical profile. Ottawa: Statistics Canada, No. 85–224–XIE au catalogue.

Canadian Council on Social Development and Family Service Canada (2003). *Canadian children's exposure to violence: What it means for parents.* Summary report. Ottawa: CCSD & Family Service Canada.

Canadian Panel on Violence Against Women (1993). *Final report of the Canadian panel on violence against women: Changing the landscape; ending violence — achieving equality*. Ottawa: Ministry of Supply and Services.

Caplan, P. (1985). *The myth of women's masochism*. New York: E.P. Dutton.

Caplan, P. & Caplan, J.B. (1999). *Thinking critically about research on sex and gender* (2nd ed.). Don Mills, ON: Longman.

Carlson, B.E., McNutt, L. & Choi, D.Y. (2003). Childhood and adult abuse among women in primary healthcare: Effects on mental health. *Journal of Interpersonal Violence, 18*, 924–941.

Carty, L. & Brand, D. (1988). Visible minority women: A creation of the Canadian state. *Resources for Feminist Research, 17*, 39–42.

Cattaneo, L.B. & Goodman, L.A. (2003). Victim-reported risk factors for continued abusive behaviour: Assessing the dangerousness of arrested batterers. *Journal of Community Psychology, 31*, 349–369.

Chamberland, C. (2003). *Violence parentale et violence conjugale: Des réalités plurielles, multidimensionnelles et interreliées*. Québec: Presses de l'Université du Québec.

Cohen, L. & Felson, M. (1979). Social change and crime rate trends: A routine activities approach. *American Sociological Review, 44*, 588–608.

Coleman, W. & Skogstad, G. (Eds.) (1990). *Policy communities and public policy in Canada*. Toronto: Copp Clark Pittman.

Comack, E. (1993). *Feminist engagement with the law: The legal recognition of the battered woman syndrome*. The CRIAW papers. Ottawa: Canadian Research Institute for the Advancement of Women.

Comack, E., Chopyk, V. & Wood, L. (2000). *Mean streets? The social locations, gender dynamics and patterns of violent crime in Winnipeg*. Winnipeg, MB: Canadian Centre for Policy Alternatives.

Crawford, M. & Gartner, R. (1992). *Women killing: Intimate femicide in Ontario 1974–1990*. Toronto: Women We Honour Action Committee.

CRIAW. (2002). *Women's experience of racism: How race and gender interact*. Retrieved August 10, 2004, from http://www.criaw-icref.ca/indexFrame_e.htm

CRIAW. (2004). *Integrated feminist analysis*. Forum held on February 20–22, 2004, Ottawa Canada. Retrieved from http://www.criaw-icref.ca/index Frame_e.htm

Daly, M. & Wilson, M. (1988). *Homicide*. New York: Adeline de Gruyter.

Daly, M. & Wilson, M. (1992). Till death do us part. In J. Radford & D. Russell (Eds.), *Femicide: The politics of woman-killing* (pp. 83-98). New York: Twayne.

DasGupta, T. (1994a). Political economy of gender, race and class: Looking at South Asian immigrant women in Canada. *Canadian Ethnic Studies, 26.*

DasGupta, T. (1994b). Multicultural policy: A terrain of struggle for immigrant women. *Canadian Women Studies/Les Cahiers de la Femme, 14,* 72–75.

DeKeseredy, W.S. & Ellis, D. (1995). Intimate violence against women in Canada. In J. Ross (Ed.), *Violence in Canada: Sociopolitical perspectives.* Toronto: Oxford University Press.

DeKeseredy, W.S. & MacLeod, L. (1997). *Woman abuse: A sociological story.* Toronto: Harcourt Brace.

Derogatis, L.R. (1993). *Brief symptom inventory: Administration, scoring, and procedures manual.* N.p.: NCS Assessment.

Des Jarlais, D.C., Friedman, S.R., Choopanya, K., Vanichseni, S. & Ward, T.P. (1992). International epidemiology of HIV and AIDS among injecting drug users. *aids, 6,* 1053–1068.

Dewhurst, A.M., Moore, R.J. & Alfano, D.P. (1992). Aggression against women by men: Sexual and spousal assault. *Journal of Offender Rehabilitation, 18,* 39–47.

Dewhurst, A.M. & Nielsen, K.M. (1997). *A review of the literature regarding risk assessment and battered women.* Position paper developed for the Edmonton Council Against Family Violence. Edmonton, AB: Edmonton Council Against Family Violence.

Dijkstra, B. (1996). *Evil sisters: The threat of female sexuality in twentieth-century culture.* New York: Henry Holt and Co.

Dobash, R.E. & Dobash, R.P. (1998). *Rethinking violence against women.* Thousand Oaks, CA: Sage Publications.

Dobash, R.E., Dobash, R.P., Cavanagh, K. & Lewis, R. (2000). *Changing violent men.* Newbury Park, CA: Sage Publications.

Doherty, D. & Hornosty, J. (2004). Abuse in a rural and farm context. In M.L. Stirling, C.A. Cameron, N. Nason-Clark & B. Miedema (Eds.), *Understanding abuse: Partnering for change* (pp. 55–82). Toronto: University of Toronto Press.

Dolon, R., Hendricks, J. & Meagher, S. (1986). Police practices and attitudes toward domestic violence. *Journal of Police Science and Administration, 14,* 187–192.

Dubois, W.E.B. (1998). *The soul of black folk.* Upper Saddle River, N.J.: Prentice Hall.

Duffy, A. & Momirov, J. (1997). *Family violence: A Canadian introduction.* Toronto: Lorimer.

Duffy, A. & Momirov, J. (2000). Family violence: Issues and advances at the end of the twentieth century. In N. Mandell & A. Duffy (Eds.), *Canadian families. Diversity, conflict, and change* (pp. 290–322). Toronto: Harcourt Canada Ltd.

Duncan, H. (2003). Social inclusion, social capital and immigration. *Canadian Issues/Themes Canadiens, 25,* 30–34.

Dutton, D. & Golant, S.K. (1995). *The batterer: A psychological profile.* New York: Basic Books.

Dutton, M.A. (1992). *Healing the trauma of woman battering: Assessment and intervention.* New York: Springer.

Ericson, R.V. & Baranek, P.M. (1982). *The ordering of justice: A study of accused persons as dependants in the criminal process.* Toronto: University of Toronto Press.

Essed, P. (1991). *Everyday racism.* Newbury Park, CA: Sage Publications.

Essed, P. (2001). *The intersection of race, gender and class.* Paper presented at the panel discussion in the 47th Session of the United Nations Commission on the Status of Women, New York, March 9, 2001.

Falmagne, R.J. (2000). Positionality and thought: On the gendered foundations of thought, culture and development. In P. H. Miller & E.K. Scholnick (Eds.), *Toward a feminist developmental psychology* (pp. 191–213). New York: Routledge.

Fanon, F. (1963). *The wretched of the earth.* New York: Grove Press.

Ferguson, K.E. (1984). *The feminist case against bureaucracy.* Philadelphia: Temple University Press.

Ferraro, K.J. (1989). Policing woman battering. *Social Problems, 36,* 61–74.

Figley, C.F. (Ed.) (2002). *Treating compassion fatigue.* Psychosocial Stress Series. New York: Brunner-Routledge.

Finn, P. & Colson, S. (1998). Civil protection orders: Legislation, current court practice, and enforcement. In *Legal interventions in family violence: Research findings and policy implications.* N.p.: U.S. Dept. of Justice. (NCJ 171666) [on-line at: http://www.ncjrs.org/pdffiles/171666. pdf].

Flanzer, J.P. (1993). Alcohol and other drugs are key causal agents of violence. In R.J. Gelles & D.R. Loseke (Eds.), *Current controversies on family violence* (pp. 171–181). Newbury Park, CA: Sage Publications.

Frank, S. (1992). Family violence in Aboriginal communities. Victoria, B.C.:

Ministry of Women's Equality.

Friday, P., Metzgar, S. & Walters, D. (1991). Policing domestic violence: Perceptions, experience, and reality. *Criminal Justice Review, 16*, 198–213.

Galabuzi, G.E. (2004). Social exclusion. In D. Raphael (Ed.), *Social determinants of health* (pp. 235-251). Toronto: Canadian Scholars Press.

Gelles, R.J. (1976). Abused wives: Why do they stay? *Journal of Marriage and the Family, 38*, 659–668.

Gelles, R.J. (1993). Through a sociological lens: Social structure and family violence. In R.J. Gelles & D.R. Loseke (Eds.), *Current controversies on family violence* (pp. 31–46). Newbury Park, CA: Sage Publications.

Gelles, R.J. (1997). *Intimate violence in families.* Newbury Park, CA: Sage Publications.

Gelles, R.J. & Strauss, M.A. (1979). Determinants of violence in the family: Toward a theoretical integration. In W.R. Burr, R. Hill, F.I. Nye & I.L. Reiss (Eds.), *Contemporary theories about the family* (pp. 549–581). New York: The Free Press.

Ghent, W., Da Sylva, N. & Farren, M. (1985). Family violence: Guidelines for recognition and management. *Canadian Medical Association Journal, 132*, 541–553.

Giles-Sims, J. (1983). *Wife-battering: A systems theory approach.* New York: Guilford Press.

Goldberg, T.G. (1990). The social formation of racist discourse. In T.G. Goldberg (Ed.), *Anatomy of racism* (pp. 295–318). Minneapolis: University of Minnesota Press.

Gondolf, E.W. (1998). *Assessing woman battering in mental health services.* Thousand Oaks, CA: Sage Publications.

Gondolf, E.W. & Fisher, E. (1988). *Battered women as survivors: An alternative to treating learned helplessness.* Lexington, MA: Lexington.

Goodman, L.A., Koss, M.P., Fitzgerald, L.F., Russo, N.F. & Keita, G.P. (1993). Male violence against women: Current research and future directions. *American Psychologist, 48*, 1054–1058.

Gorkoff, K. & Runner, J. (Eds.) (2003). *Being heard: The experiences of young women in prostitution.* Halifax: Fernwood Publishing.

Greene, B. (1995). Institutional racism in the mental health professions. In J. Adleman & G. Enguidanos (Eds.), *Racism in the lives of women: Testimony, theory and guide to antiracist practice* (pp. 113–125). New York: Haworth Press.

Guillaumin, C. (1995). *Racism, sexism, power, and ideology.* London: Routledge.

Hamberger, L.K. & Ambuel, B. (1997). Training psychology students and professionals to recognize and intervene in partner violence: Borrowing a page from medicine. *Psychotherapy, 34,* 375–385.

Hamilton, A.C. & Sinclair, C.M. (1991). Chapter 13: Aboriginal women. *The inquiry and the issues: Report of the Aboriginal justice inquiry of Manitoba.* The Justice System and Aboriginal People, Vol. 1. Winnipeg, MB: Queen's Printer.

Hanson, R.K. & Bussière, M.T. (1998). Predicting relapse: A meta-analysis of sexual offender recidivism studies. *Journal of Consulting and Clinical Psychology, 66,* 348–362.

Harrison, D. (2000). Violence in the military community. In L. Beaman (Ed.), *New perspectives on deviance: The construction of deviance in everyday life* (pp. 246–262). Scarborough, ON: Prentice Hall.

Harrison, D. (2004). The Canadian forces response to woman abuse in military. In M.L. Stirling, C.A. Cameron, N. Nason-Clark & B. Miedema (Eds.), *Understanding abuse. Partnering for change* (pp. 155–194). Toronto: University of Toronto Press.

Henning, K. & Feder, L. (2004). A comparison of men and women arrested for domestic violence: Who presents the greater threat? *Journal of Family Violence, 29,* 69–80.

Hiebert-Murphy, D. & Burnside, L. (Eds.) (2001). *Pieces of a puzzle: Perspectives on child sexual abuse.* Nova Scotia & Manitoba: Fernwood Publishing & RESOLVE.

Homant, R.J. & Kennedy, D.B. (1985). Police perceptions of spouse abuse: A comparison of male and female officers. *Journal of Criminal Justice, 13,* 29–47.

Hornosty, J. & Doherty, D. (2002). *Responding to wife abuse in farm and rural communities: Searching for solutions that work.* Regina, SK: Saskatchewan Institute of Public Policy.

Hotaling, G.T. & Sugarman, D.B. (1990). A risk marker analysis of assaulted wives. *Journal of Family Violence, 5,* 1–13.

Jaaber, R.A. & Dasgupta, S. (n.d.). *Assessing social risks of battered women.* Retrieved June 2, 2004, from http://data.ipharos.com/praxis/documents/AssessingSocialRisk.pdf

Jaffe, P., Reitzel, D., Hastings, E. & Austin, G. (1991). *Wife assault as a crime: The perspectives of victims and police officers on a charging policy in London, Ontario, from 1980–1990.* London Family Court Clinic Inc., Department of Justice Canada, Working Document [WD 1991–13A], April 1991.

Jasinski, J.L. (2001). Theoretical explanations for violence against women. In C. M. Renzetti, J. L. Edleson & R. K. Bergen (Eds.), *Sourcebook on violence against women* (pp. 5–22). Thousand Oaks, CA: Sage Publications.

Javed, N. (2002). *Taking our health in our hands: Immigrant and visible minority women's perspective on the health determinants.* Paper presented at the 9th International Women's Health Meeting, York University, Toronto, Ontario, Canada.

Jiwani, Y. (1997). *Violence is about power.* Retrieved March 22, 2004, http://www.harbour.stu.ca/freda/articles/power.htm.

Johnson, H. (1996). *Dangerous domains: Violence against women in Canada.* Toronto: Nelson Canada.

Johnson, H. (2000a). Violence against women: A special topic survey. In R.A. Silverman, J.J. Teevan & V.F. Sacco (Eds.), *Crime in Canadian society* (pp. 118–127). Toronto: Harcourt Brace.

Johnson, H. (2000b). Responding to domestic abuse. In J.V. Roberts (Ed.), *Criminal justice in Canada: A reader* (pp. 245–258). Toronto: Harcourt Brace.

Johnson, I.M. & Sigler, R.T. (1995). Community attitudes: A study of definitions and punishment of spouse abusers and child abusers. *Journal of Criminal Justice, 23,* 477–487.

Kaufman, G. Jr. (1992). The mysterious disappearance of battered women in family therapists' offices: Male privilege colluding with male violence. *Journal of Marriage and the Family, 18,* 233–243.

Kaufman Kantor, G. & Jasinski, J.L. (1998). Dynamics and risk factors in partner violence. In J.L. Jasinski & L. Williams (Eds.), *Partner violence: A comprehensive review of 20 years of research* (pp. 1–43). Thousand Oaks, CA: Sage Publications.

Kempe, C.H. (1962). The battered child syndrome. *Journal of the American Medical Association, 181,* 107–112.

Kimmer, E.B. & Crawford, M. (Eds.) (1999). *Innovations in feminist psychological research.* New York: Cambridge University Press.

Kragh, J.R. & Huber, C.H. (2002). Family resilience and domestic violence:

Panacea or pragmatic therapeutic perspective? *The Journal of Individual Psychology, 58,* 290–304.

Kropp, P.R., Hart, S., Webster, C. & Eaves, D. (1995). *Manual for the spousal assault risk assessment guide* (2nd ed.). Vancouver: The British Columbia Institute on Family Violence.

Labonte, R. (2004). Social inclusion/exclusion and health: Dancing the dialectic. In D. Raphael (Ed.), *Social determinants of health* (pp. 253–266). Toronto: Canadian Scholars Press.

LaPrairie, C. (1996). "Examining Aboriginal Corrections in Canada." Solicitor General Canada; APC 14 CA.

LaRocque, E. (1995). Violence in Aboriginal communities. In M. Valverde, L. MacLeod & K. Johnston (Eds.), *Wife assault and the Canadian criminal justice system* (pp. 104–124). Toronto: Centre of Criminology, University of Toronto.

Larouche, G. (1987). *Agir contre la violence.* Montréal: La pleine lune.

Lawrentz, F., Lembo, J.F. & Schade, T. (1988). Time series analysis of the effect of a domestic violence directive on the number of arrests per day. *Journal of Criminal Justice, 16,* 493–498.

Light, L. & Rivkin, S. (1994). *Power, control and violence in family relationships: The challenges of a justice system response.* Paper presented at Today's Families: A Bridge to the Future Conference, B.C. Ministry of Attorney General and Justice Institute of B.C.

Lupri, E., Grandin, E. & Merlin, M.B. (1994). Socioeconomic status and male violence in the Canadian homes: A re-examination. *Canadian Journal of Sociology, 19,* 47–73.

Macbeth-Williams, T. (Ed.) (1986). *The impact of television: A naturalistic experiment in three communities.* New York: Academic Press.

MacLeod, L. (1980). *Wife battering in Canada: The vicious circle.* Ottawa: Canadian Advisory Council on the Status of Women.

MacLeod, L. & Kinnon, D. (1996). *Taking the next step to stop woman abuse: From violence prevention to individual, family, community and societal health: A practical vision of collaborative change.* Ottawa: National Clearinghouse on Family Violence.

Mahon, P. (1995). *Changing perspectives: A case study of intimate partner homicides in Nova Scotia.* Halifax: St. Francis Xavier University, Family Violence Prevention Division & Health Canada.

Mann, R. (2000). *Who owns domestic abuse? The local politics of a social problem.* Toronto: University of Toronto Press.

Martin, A.J., Berenson, K.R., Griffing, S., Sage, R.E., Madry, L., Bingham, L.E. & Primm, B.J. (2000). The process of leaving an abusive relationship: The role of risk assessments and decision-certainty. *Journal of Family Violence, 15,* 109–122.

Martin, G. (1996). La recherche sur la violence envers les femmes. In H. Dagenais (Ed.), *Science, conscience et action: Vingt-cinq ans de recherche féministe au Québec* (pp. 121–148). Montréal: Les éditions du remue-ménage.

Martin, M.E. (1997). Double your trouble: Dual arrest in family violence. *Journal of Family Violence, 12,* 139–157.

Martz, F. & Saraurer, B. (2000). *Domestic violence and the experiences of rural women in east central Saskatchewan.* Saskatoon: Prairie Women's Health Centre of Excellence. Retrieved June 20, 2002 from http://www.pwhce.ca/pdf/domestic-viol.pdf

McCall, G. (1993). Risk factors and sexual assault prevention. *Journal of Interpersonal Violence, 8,* 277–295.

McGillivray, A. & Comaskey, B. (1996). *Intimate violence, aboriginal women and justice system response: A Winnipeg study.* Manitoba: RESOLVE.

McGillivray, A. & Comasky, B. (1999). The criminal justice system. In A. McGillivray (Ed.), *Black eyes all of the time: Intimate violence, Aboriginal women and the justice system* (pp. 84–113). Toronto: University of Toronto Press.

McGillivray, A. & Parisienne, J. (1997). *Intimate violence, Aboriginal women and justice system response: An annotated bibliography.* Manitoba: RESOLVE.

McIvor, S. & Nahanee, T. (1998). Aboriginal women: Invisible victims of violence. In K. Bonneycastle & G. Rigakos (Eds.), *Unsettling truths* (pp. 63–72). Vancouver: Collective Press.

McLeod, L. (1995). *Desperately seeking certainty: Assessing and reducing the risk of harm for women who are abused.* A discussion paper prepared for the Alberta Advisory Council on Women's Issues. Edmonton: Alberta Advisory Council on Women's Issues.

Meldrum, L., King, R. & Spooner, D. (2002). Secondary traumatic stress in case managers working in community mental health services. In C.L. Figley (Ed.), *Treating compassion fatigue.* Psychosocial Stress Series (pp. 85–106). New York: Brunner-Routledge.

Miedema, B. & Nason-Clark, N. (2004). Introduction. In M.L. Stirling, C.A. Cameron, N. Nason-Clark & B. Miedema (Eds.), *Understanding abuse: Partnering for change* (pp. 3–19). Toronto: University of Toronto Press.

Mignon, S.I. & Holmes, W.M. (1995). Police response to mandatory arrest laws. *Crime and Delinquency, 41*, 430–442.

Miles, R. (1989). *Racism.* London & New York: Routledge.

Mills, L. (1996). Empowering battered women transnationally: The case for postmodern interventions. *Social Work, 41*, 261–268.

Minaker, J. (2001). Evaluating criminal justice response to intimate abuse through the lens of women's needs. *Canadian Journal of Women and the Law, 13*, 74–106.

Minh-Ha, T. (1993). All-owning spectatorship. In S. Gumew & A. Yeatman (Eds.), *Feminism and the politics of difference* (pp. 157–176). Halifax: Fernwood Publishing.

Mohammaj, H., Bose, A., Javed, N., Lee, J. & Martin, L. (2004). *The impact of the National Security Agenda on racialized women bringing us out of the policy the ghetto and into the developments of national policy: Strategies and solutions.* Unpublished research report, Canadian Institute of Research for the Advancement of Women & the National Organization of Immigrant and visible Minority Women of Canada. Retrieved from http://www.criaw-icref.ca/indexFrame_e.htm.

Molden, J. (2002). Rewriting stories: Women's responses to the Safe Journey Group. In L.M. Tutty & C. Goard (Eds.), *Reclaiming self: Issues and resources for women abused by intimate partners* (pp. 81–97). Nova Scotia & Manitoba: Fernwood Publishing & RESOLVE.

Morris, M. (2002). *Participatory action research: A guide to becoming a researcher for social change.* Ontario: Canadian Research Institute for the Advancement of Women.

Narayan, U. (1997). *Dislocating culture: Identities, traditions and third world feminism.* New York & London: Routledge.

Native Women's Association of Canada (1991). *Voices of Aboriginal women: Aboriginal women speak out about violence.* Ottawa: Canadian Council on Social Development.

National Clearinghouse on Family Violence (1993). *Gender and violence in the mass media.* Ottawa: Health Canada.

National Clearinghouse on Family Violence (1995). *Woman abuse.* Ottawa: Health Canada.

National Clearinghouse on Family Violence (2000). *Counselling programs for men who are violent in relationships.* Ottawa: Health Canada.

Ng, R. (1993). Sexism, racism and Canadian nationalism. In S. Gumew & A. Yeatman, (Eds.), *Feminism and the politics of difference* (pp. 197–211). Halifax: Fernwood Publishing.

Nixon, K. (2002). Leave him or lose them? The child protection response to woman abuse. In L.M. Tutty & C. Goard (Eds.). *Reclaiming self: Issues and resources for women abused by intimate partners* (pp. 64–80). Nova Scotia & Manitoba: Fernwood Publishing & RESOLVE.

Nuffield, J. (1998). Issues in urban corrections for Aboriginal people: Report on a focus group and an overview of the literature and experience. The Ministry of the Solicitor General of Canada: APC 17. [on-line at: http://www.sgc.gc.ca/epub/abocor/e199803/e199803.htm]

O'Connor, M.F. (2001). On the etiology an effective management of professional distress and impairment among psychologists. *Professional psychology: Research and practice, 32*, 345–350.

Okun, L. (1988). Termination or resumption of cohabitation in woman battering relationships: A statistical study. In G. Hotaling, D. Finkelhor, J. Kirkpatrick & M. Straus (Eds.), *Coping with family violence: Research and policy perspectives* (pp. 107–119). Newbury Park, CA: Sage Publications.

O'Leary, K.D. (1993). Through a psychological lens: Personality traits, personality disorders, and levels of violence. In R.J. Gelles & D.R. Loseke (Eds.), *Current controversies on family violence* (pp. 7–30). Newbury Park, CA: Sage Publications.

Ontario Native Women's Association (1989). *Breaking free: A proposal for change to Aboriginal family violence.* Thunder Bay, ON.

Outlaw, L. (1990). Toward a critical theory of race. In D.T. Goldberg (Ed.), *Anatomy of racism* (pp. 58–82). Minneapolis: University of Minnesota Press.

Pagelow, M.D. (1992). Adult victims of domestic violence. *Journal of Interpersonal Violence, 7*, 87–120.

Pearlman, L. A. (1999). Self-care for trauma therapists: Ameliorating vicarious traumatization. In B. Hudnall Stamm (Ed.), *Secondary traumatic stress: Self-care issues for clinicians, researchers and educators* (pp. 51–64).

Baltimore: Sidran Institute and Press.

Pedlar, D. (1991). *Domestic violence: Review into the administration of justice in Manitoba.* Winnipeg, MB: Queens Printer.

Pence, E. (1984). Response to Peter Neidig's article: 'Women's shelters, men's collectives and other issues in the field of spouse abuse.' *Victimology, 9,* 477–482.

Pence, E. (1988). Batterer programs: Shifting from community collusion to community confrontation. In P.L. Caesar and L.K. Hamberger (Eds.), *Treating men who batter: Theory, practice and programs.* New York: Springer.

Pense, E. & Paymar, M. (1986). *Power and control: Tactics of men who batter.* Duluth, MN: Minnesota Program Development Inc.

Pithers, W.D., Marques, J.K., Gibat, C.C. & Marlatt, G. (1983). Relapse prevention with sexual aggressives: A self-control model of treatment and the maintenance of change. In J.G. Greer & I.R. Stuart (Eds.), *The sexual aggressor: Current perspectives on treatment* (pp. 214–234). New York: Van Nostrand Reinhold.

Podnieks, E. (1988). Elder abuse: It's time we did something about it. In B. Schlesinger & R. Schlesinger (Eds.), *Abuse of elderly: Issues and annotated bibliography* (pp. 32–44). Toronto: University of Toronto Press.

Pope, K.S., Butcher, J. & Selen, J. (1994). *The MMPI-1, MMPI-2, and MMPI-C in court: A pratical guide for expert witnesses and attorneys.* Washington, DC: American Psychological Association.

Prochaska, J.O., DiClemente, C.C. & Norcross, J.C. (1992). In search of how people change: Applications to addictive behavior. *American Psychologist, 47,* 1102–1114.

Prochaska, J.O., Norcross, J.C. & DiClemente, C.C. (1994). *Changing for good: A revolutionary six stage program for overcoming bad habits and moving your life positively forward.* New York: Avon Books.

Prochaska, J.O., Velicer, W.F., Rossi, J.S., Goldstein, M.G., Marcus, B.H., Rakowski, W., Fiore, C., Harlow, L.L., Redding, C.A., Rosenbloom, D. & Rossi, S.R. (1994). Stages of change and decisional balance for 12 problem behaviors. *American Psychologist, 13,* 39–46.

Proulx, J. & Perrault, S. (Eds.) (2000). *No place for violence: Canadian Aboriginal alternatives.* Halifax: Fernwood Publishing.

Radford, J. (1992). Where do we go from here. In J. Radford & D.E.H. Russell

(Eds.), *Femicide: The politics of woman killing* (pp. 351–357). New York: Twayne.

Radford, J. & Russell, D.E.H. (Eds.) (1992). *Femicide: The politics of woman killing.* New York: Twayne.

Richardson, J.I. (2001). *Guidebook on vicarious trauma: Recommended solutions for anti-violence workers.* N.p.: Health Canada, Family Violence Prevention Unit.

Riger, S., Raja, S. & Camacho, J. (2002). The radiating impact of intimate partner violence. *Journal of Interpersonal Violence, 17,* 184–205.

Riggs, D.S., Caulfield, M.B. & Street, A.E. (2000). Risk for domestic violence: Factors associated with perpetration and victimization. *Journal of Clinical Psychology, 56,* 1289–1316.

Rinfret-Raynor, M., Paquet-Deehy, A., Larouche, G. & Cantin, S. (1992). *Intervening with battered women: Evaluating the effectiveness of a feminist model.* Montreal: Editions St-Martin.

Roberts, A.R. (2002). Myths, facts, and realities regarding battered women and their children: An overview. In A.R. Roberts (Ed.), *Handbook of domestic violence intervention strategies: Policies, programs, and legal remedies* (pp. 3–21). New York: Oxford University Press

Robertson, A. (1998). *Violence against women in rural areas: A search for understanding.* University of Saskatchewan: Master's thesis.

Rodgers, K. (1994). Wife assault: The findings of a national survey. *Juristat Service Bulletin: Canadian Centre for Justice Studies, 14,* 1–21. Ottawa, ON: Minister of Industry, Science and Technology.

Rosenbaum, A., Hoge, S., Adelman S., Warnken, W., Fletcher, K. & Kane, R. (1994). Head injury in partner-abusive men. *Journal of Consulting and Clinical Psychology, 62,* 1187–1193.

Rothery, M., Tutty, L. & Weaver, G. (1999). Tough choices: Women, abusive partners and the ecology of decision-making. *Canadian Journal of Community Mental Health, 18,* 5–18.

Rubin, H.J. & Rubin, I.S. (1995). *Qualitative interviewing: The art of hearing data.* Thousand Oaks, CA: Sage Publications.

Saakvitne, K.W. & Pearlman, L.A. (1996). *Transforming the pain: A workbook on vicarious trauma for helping professionals who work with traumatized clients.* New York: W. W. Norton & Company.

Said, E.W. (1979). *Orientalism*. New York: Vintage Books.

Salazar, L.F., Baker, C.K., Price, A.W. & Carlin, K. (2003). Moving beyond the individual: Examining the effects of domestic violence policies on social norms. *American Journal of Community Psychology, 32*, 253–264.

Schwartz, M.D. & Pitts, V. (1995). Toward a feminist routine activities theory on campus sexual assault. *Justice Quarterly, 12*, 9–31.

Sheeny, E. (1999). Legal responses to violence against women in Canada. *Canadian Women's Studies, 19*, 62–104.

Sheffield, C.J. (1989). The invisible intruder: Women's experiences of obscene phone calls. *Gender and Society, 3*, 483–488.

Simon, T.B., Anderson, M., Thompson, M.P., Crosby, A.E., Shelley, B. & Sacks, J.J. (2001). Attitudinal acceptance of intimate partner violence among U.S. adults. *Violence and Victims, 16*, 115–126.

Smith, E. (2004). *Nowhere to turn: Responding to partner violence against immigrant and visible minority women: Voices of frontline workers*. Ottawa: Canadian Council on Social Development.

Snider, L. (1998). Struggles for justice: Criminalization and alternatives. In K. Bonneycastle & G. Rigakos (Eds.), *Unsettling Truths*. Vancouver: Collective Press.

Stalans, L.J. (1996). Family harmony or individual protection? *American Behavioral Scientist, 39*, 433–449.

Stamm, B.H. (2002). Measuring compassion satisfaction as well as fatigue: Developmental history of the compassion satisfaction and fatigue test. In Figley, C.F. (Ed.), *Treating compassion fatigue*. Psychosocial Stress Series (pp. 107–119). New York: Brunner-Routlege.

Stamm, B.H. (Ed.) (1999). *Secondary traumatic stress: Self-care issues for clinicians, researchers, & educators*. Baltimore, MD: Sidran Institute and Press.

Stark, E. (1993). Mandatory arrest of batterers: A reply to its critics. *American Behavioral Scientist, 36*, 6651–680.

Statistics Canada (1996). *1996 Census*. Ottawa: Statistics Canada.

Statistics Canada (1998). *Family violence in Canada: A statistical profile, 1998*.

Statistics Canada (1999). *General social survey on victimization*.

Statistics Canada (1999). *Homicide in Canada*. Ottawa: Canadian Centre for Justice.

Statistics Canada (1999/2000). *Transition home survey*.

Statistics Canada (2000). *National transition house survey*.

Statistics Canada (2001). *Family violence in Canada: A statistical profile, 2001.*

Statistics Canada (2003). *Family violence in Canada: A statistical profile, 2003.*

Statistics Canada (2004). *Family violence in Canada: A statistical profile, 2004.*

Status of Women (2002). *Assessing violence against women: A statistical profile.* Ottawa: Status of Women Canada.

Stirling, M.L., Cameron, C.A., Nason-Clark, N. & Miedema, M. (2004). *Understanding abuse: Partnering for change.* Toronto: University of Toronto Press.

Strange, C. (1995). Historical perspective on wife assault. In M. Valverde, L. MacLeod & K. Johnson (Eds.), *Wife assault and the Canadian criminal justice system.* (pp.???). Toronto: Centre of Criminology, University of Toronto.

Strauss, A. & Corbin, J. (1998). *Basics of qualitative research: Grounded theory procedures and techniques.* Newbury Park, CA: Sage Publications.

Timmins, L. (1995). *Listening to the thunder. Advocates talk about the battered women's movement.* Vancouver: Women's Research Centre.

Tremblay, R. (2000). The origins of youth violence. *Isuma, 1,* 19–24.

Tutty, L. (1998). Mental health issues of abused women: The perceptions of shelter workers. *Canadian Journal of Community Mental Health, 17,* 79–102.

Tutty, L. (1999). Considering emotional abuse in the link between spouse and child abuse. *Journal of Emotional Abuse, 1,* 53–79.

Tutty, L. (1999). *Domestic violence involving firearms in Alberta: Case studies of women and children.* Final research report to The Canadian Firearms Centre, Department of Justice Canada.

Tutty, L.M. & Goard, C. (2002). Challenges and future directions. In L.M. Tutty & C. Goard (Eds.), *Reclaiming self: Issues and resources for women abused by intimate partners* (pp. 117–129). Nova Scotia & Manitoba: Fernwood Publishing & RESOLVE.

Tutty, L.M. & Goard, C. (Eds.) (2002). *Reclaiming self: Issues and resources for women abused by intimate partners.* Nova Scotia & Manitoba: Fernwood Publishing & RESOLVE.

Tutty, L.M. & Goard, C. (2002). Woman abuse in Canada: An overview. In L.M. Tutty & C. Goard (Eds.), *Reclaiming self: Issues and resources for women abused by intimate partners* (pp. 10–24). Nova Scotia & Manitoba: Fernwood Publishing & RESOLVE.

Tutty, L.M. & Rothery, M. (2002). How well do emergency shelters assist women and their children? In L.M. Tutty & C. Goard (Eds.), *Reclaiming self: Issues and resources for women abused by intimate partners* (pp. 25–42). Nova Scotia & Manitoba: Fernwood Publishing & RESOLVE.

Ursel, J. (1992). *Private lives, public policy: 100 years of state intervention in the family.* Toronto: Women's Press.

Ursel, J. (2002). "His sentence is my freedom": Processing domestic violence cases in the Winnipeg family violence court. In L.M. Tutty & C. Goard (Eds.), *Reclaiming self: Issues and resources for women abused by intimate partners* (pp. 43–63). Nova Scotia & Manitoba: Fernwood Publishing & RESOLVE.

Ursel, J. (2002). Zero tolerance under scrutiny. *Resolve News, 4,* 1–6.

Ursel, J. & Brickey, S. (1996). The potential of legal reform reconsidered: A case study of the Manitoba zero tolerance policy on family violence. In T. O'Reilly-Fleming (Ed.), *Post Critical Criminology* (pp. ??–??). Scarborough, ON: Prentice Hall.

Van Brunschot, E. (2000). Assault stories. In R.A. Silverman, J.J. Teevan & V.F. Sacco (Eds.), *Crime in Canadian society* (pp. 140–147). Toronto: Hartcourt Brace.

Van der Put, D. (1990). Literature review on Aboriginal victims of crime. The Public Inquiry into the Administration of Justice and Aboriginal People.

Van Manen, M. (1990). *Researching lived experience.* London, ON: Althouse Press.

Walker, L. (1984). *The battered woman syndrome.* New York: Springer.

Walker, L. (1991). Post-traumatic stress disorder in women: Diagnosis and treatment of battered woman syndrome. *Psychotherapy, 28,* 21–29.

Walker, L.E.A. (1993). The battered woman syndrome is a psychological consequence of abuse. In R.J. Gelles & D.R. Loseke (Eds.), *Current controversies on family violence* (pp. 133–153). Newbury Park, CA: Sage Publications.

Walker, L.E.A. (1999). Psychology and domestic violence around the world. *American Psychologist, 54,* 21–29.

Ward, T., Louden, K., Hudson S.M. & Marshall, W.L. (1995). A descriptive model of the offense change for child molesters. *Journal of Interpersonal Violence, 10,* 452–472.

Warshaw, C. (1989). Limitations of the medical model in the care of battered women. *Gender and Society, 3,* 506–517.

Weisz, A.N., Tolman, R.M. & Saunders, D.G. (2000). Assessing the risk of severe domestic violence: The importance of survivors' predictions. *Journal of Interpersonal Violence, 15*, 75–90.

Whalen, M. (1996). *Counseling to end violence against women: A subversive model.* Thousand Oaks, CA: Sage Publications.

Wharf, B. & McKenzie, B. (1998). *Connecting policy to practice in the human services.* Toronto: Oxford University Press.

Worden, A.P. (2000). The changing boundaries of the criminal justice system: Redefining the problem and the response in domestic violence. In *Boundary Changes in Criminal Justice Organizations.* [on-line at: http://www.ncjrs.org/criminal_justice2000/vol_2/02g2.pdf]

Worden, A. (2000). Models of community coordination in partner violence cases. Final report (draft) submitted to the U.S. Department of Justice, National Institute of Justice Grant no. NIJ 95-WT-NX-0006.

Wolfe, D.A., Crooks, C.V., Lee, V., McIntyre-Smith, A. & Jaffe, P.G. (2003). The effects of children's exposure to domestic violence: A meta-analysis and critique. *Clinical Child and Family Psychology Review, 6*, 171–187.

Yllo, K.A. (1993). Through a feminist lens: Gender, power, and violence. In R.J. Gelles & D.R. Loseke (Eds.), *Current controversies on family violence* (pp. 47–62). Newbury Park, CA: Sage Publications.

York, G. (1992). *The dispossessed: Life and death in Native Canada.* Boston: Little Brown.

About the Authors

SHARON BUTALA is the author of 14 books of both fiction and nonfiction, the 15th of which (*Lilac Moon: Dreaming of the Real West*) was published by HarperCollins Canada in April, 2005. In 2002 she became an Officer of the Order of Canada.

ANN MARIE DEWHURST is a clinical and forensic psychologist. She is currently working on her doctoral dissertation, a qualitative study of the experience of being an ethical psychologist. Ann Marie teaches courses in Women's Studies and Psychology for Athabasca University. She is also a chartered psychologist in private practice with Valerian Consulting Ltd. She works primarily with people who have been abusive and her focus is family reintegration.

DEB FARDEN is a registered psychologist who has worked in Saskatoon for over 20 years. She worked in a women's shelter for seven years and facilitated domestic abuse programs for women for 13 years. Both her Honours thesis and her Master's thesis focused on violence against women in intimate relationships. She is currently working in a program for men who wish to stop their violence against their intimate female partners. Since 1998 she has participated in ongoing education in psychodramatic bodywork, shiatsu, and psychodrama. She has her level one certification in psychodrama and is a certified trainer in psychodramatic bodywork. Deb has a passion for cooking and gardening, which she considers expressions of both creativity and her personal therapy.

NIKKI GERRARD is a community psychologist and the Coordinator of the Rural Quality of Life and Adult Counselling programs, Adult Community Mental Health Services, Saskatoon Health Region, where she is the Chief Psychologist for the Adult Services in Mental Health. She is also an adjunct professor in the Department of Community Health and Epidemiology, College of Medicine, University of Saskatchewan. Nikki designed and implemented a farm stress program over 11 years ago and has worked extensively in rural mental health. As a community psychologist, Nikki is interested in the psyche of the community and spends a lot of her time developing community strengths, through community development, education, research, and organizing. Her research interests include racism and sexism, together, in mental health systems, resiliency in rural people, and women's psychology.

CARMEN GILL holds a Ph.D. in sociology from the Université du Québec à Montréal. She is currently the Director of the Muriel McQueen Fergusson Centre for Family Violence Research at the University of New Brunswick. Her areas of expertise are the fields of family, gender, social policy, third sector and violence against women. She is involved in different SSHRC-funded research projects looking at the dynamics between the government and community-based organizations, and at the justice and community response to family violence in the prairie provinces.

MARY RUCKLOS HAMPTON holds an Ed.D. in Counselling and Consulting Psychology from Harvard University and an Ed.M. in Counselling Psychology from Boston University. She is a registered clinical psychologist in the province of Saskatchewan. Mary is a full professor of psychology at Luther College, at the University of Regina. She teaches courses in psychology of women, humanistic psychology, ethics, developmental psychology, and abnormal psychology. She has published in the areas of youth sexual health, women's reproductive health, cross-cultural psychology, and community development. Her research interests include violence against women, death and dying, women's health, and cross-cultural healing.

NAYYAR JAVED is a psychologist and social activist. She has recently retired from Adult Community Mental Health Services in Saskatoon and now has her own practice. Nayyar immigrated from Pakistan, where she was an assistant professor at Peshawar University. Nayyar has been involved in the anti-racism and feminist movements in Canada for the past 25 years. She has published book chapters, journal articles, and resource material on multiculturalism, racial and gender oppression, and feminist therapy. She has presented papers at local, national and international levels.

STEPHANIE L. MARTIN holds a B.A. in Psychology from the University of Victoria and a M.Sc. and Ph.D. in educational psychology (specialization: counselling psychology) from the University of Calgary. She is a registered doctoral psychologist and maintains a private practice emphasizing a variety of issues of concern to women and adolescents. She also holds an assistant professorship in the Department of Educational Psychology and Special Education at the University of Saskatchewan. Her teaching areas encompass the theory and practice of counselling/psychotherapy, professional practice and ethics, qualitative research methodology, and the psychology of women and gender; research interests focus on healing from trauma, particularly violence and abuse, helper development and well-being, and early intervention and prevention related to mental health concerns. Stephanie strives to incorporate a feminist-based, collaborative, action-oriented approach to practice and research.

KAREN M. NIELSEN recently completed her doctoral dissertation, a qualitative exploration of the experiences of battered women in post-secondary education. Karen teaches courses in Women's Studies and Criminology at Athabasca University. She is also a clinical social worker in private practice with Valerian Consulting Ltd. Her work is family focused with an emphasis on working with women and children recovering from family violence and trauma. She enjoys a good book and a hike in the mountains for relaxation.

LESLIE M. TUTTY is a full professor with the Faculty of Social Work at the University of Calgary, where she teaches courses in both clinical social work methods and research. Her research over the past 15 years has focused on prevention of and interventions with family violence in a variety of forms, including a number of evaluations of shelter and post-shelter programs for abused women, support groups for abused women, treatment for adult and child victims of sexual abuse, and groups for men who abuse their partners. Leslie is currently the Academic Research Coordinator of RESOLVE Alberta, a tri-provincial research institute on family violence.

JANE URSEL teaches sociology at the University of Manitoba. She is also the director of RESOLVE, a tri-provincial research network with offices at the Universities of Manitoba, Saskatchewan and Calgary. She is the principal investigator of two longitudinal studies, one of the Winnipeg Family Violence Court, and another, a tri-provincial study, entitled Women Abused by Intimate Partners. She is particularly interested in social policy focused research and is a board member of the Manitoba Law Society.

Acknowledgements

This volume was made possible because of the commitment of RESOLVE (Research and Education for Solutions to Violence and Abuse) to solicit and disseminate research that will contribute toward ending violence and abuse in our society. We thank RESOLVE for supporting this project, and especially our amazing leader, Jane Ursel, director of the RESOLVE network. She inspires us to work collaboratively for a changed society. The efforts of the RESOLVE publication committee, particularly Christine Ateah, made this volume a reality. Christine gave us respect and patience and full support in our creative process. Marc Côté of Cormorant Books has offered much helpful guidance, created a wonderful new design for this series, and has committed his many talents to this volume.

Each author has generously and courageously shared her ideas, wisdom, and heart, even when it was difficult to do so. Sharon Butala is an award-winning poet and writer who graciously gave her time and beautiful words to our project. Paula Caplan, feminist scholar, author, and social activist, devoted many hours to improving this manuscript.

Many individuals assisted with this project. Lyndsay Foster, John Hampton, Tara Lorenz, and Danielle O'Byrne (four brilliant Luther College students) provided much appreciated research, editorial, and creative support in preparing this volume. Teri Posyniak has contributed wonderful cover art to this project. We thank our families for their continued love and support. Luther College at the University of Regina and Adult Community Mental Health Services, Saskatoon Health Region gave infrastructure support and resources for the editorial preparation of this book and without which help we could never have completed this project.